RESCUING THE
EMOTIONAL LIVES OF
OVERWEIGHT
CHILDREN

RESCUING THE EMOTIONAL LIVES OF OVERWEIGHT CHILDREN

What Our Kids Go Through — And How We Can Help

by Sylvia Rimm, Ph.D.

New York Times best-selling author of *See Jane Win*

with Eric Rimm, Sc.D., Harvard School of Public Health

RODALE

Printed in the United States of America
Rodale Inc. makes every effort to use acid-free ∞, recycled paper ♻.

Illustrations by Sandy Freeman

Book design by Joanna Williams

Library of Congress Cataloging-in-Publication Data

Rimm, Sylvia B., date.
　　Rescuing the emotional lives of overweight children : what our kids go
　　through—and how we can help / by Sylvia Rimm, with Eric Rimm ;
　　foreword by Al Roker.
　　　　p.　　cm.
　　Includes index.
　　ISBN 1–57954–850–4 hardcover
　　1. Obesity in children—Psychological aspects.　2. Overweight
children—Psychology.　3. Overweight children—Mental health.
4. Obesity in children—Social aspects.　5. Body image in children.
I. Rimm, Eric.　II. Title.
RJ399.C6 R54　2004
618.92'398'0019—dc22　　　　　　　　　　　　　　　2003024478

Distributed to the book trade by St. Martin's Press

2　4　6　8　10　9　7　5　3　1　hardcover

RODALE
WE INSPIRE AND ENABLE PEOPLE TO IMPROVE
THEIR LIVES AND THE WORLD AROUND THEM

FOR MORE OF OUR PRODUCTS
WWW.RODALESTORE.COM
(800) 848-4735

Dedicated to those who shared their stories with me.

CONTENTS

FOREWORD

Growing up heavy is no fun. Take it from one who knows. For teenagers, life can be tough enough. Raging hormones, the opposite sex, added responsibilities, and more are the burdens we all carry as young people. Add the weight of being overweight to those burdens, and what should be the best time of your life can be the worst.

As an overweight teen, I endured taunts, self-doubt, ridicule, and disdain from all parties in my life, family and friends included. Some of it was intentional, some of it not. "Wow, you must be getting ready to play football, right?" "Albert doesn't miss many meals, does he?" "Jeez, you're fat!" "Hey, hey, hey! It's Fat Albert!!!"

But how do we make sure our children who are obese get healthy, both physically and emotionally? Thankfully, Sylvia Rimm takes a measured, calm, rational look at a subject that has become a national obsession and almost hysteria. What is important is that we are raising children who are secure in their self-image and their lives as much as they can be.

I wish my parents had had this book when I was growing up. It was a different time then. They did the best they could raising a "husky" boy in the 1960s and '70s. Let's face it, fat people are the last "minority" that is okay to make fun of. How many movies, television shows, and cartoons go for the cheap laugh by making fun of fat people? And when I say "minority," hey, we're 60 percent of the U.S. population. So don't tick us off. Read on and learn.

—Al Roker, NBC's *Today* show

ACKNOWLEDGMENTS

I could not have accomplished my study or this book alone. I have many individuals to thank for my findings, insights, and advice. Some permitted me to acknowledge their help, but I fear that I may have unintentionally omitted others, whose assistance I nevertheless appreciate. There were quite a few people involved who preferred that I not include their names; with respect for their privacy, I have left them off this list, although I greatly value their contributions.

First, I'd like to thank the schools that participated in my survey by providing opportunities for focus group discussions. I also want to extend my appreciation to the adolescents and adults who shared their life experiences with me and explained the pressures and problems related to their being overweight during childhood. For the most part, these interviews were stories of resilience and success.

I'm grateful to my husband, Buck, and my son, Eric, for their help with the analysis of the statistical data. It was especially wonderful to have Eric contribute an important chapter to our book. Thank you to my efficient assistants, Marilyn Knackert, Joanne Riedl, and Kari Roth, for helping with coding the data. I'd like to thank Gary Chase for his computer consultation for the survey and Adrienne Kreger-May for her assistance in gathering research. I appreciate Karen Block's assistance in designing the graphs for our book and I especially value the important and thorough work of my editorial assistant, Erika Stueber. Eric would also like to thank Jill Arnold for her editorial assistance. To my Rodale editors, Lou Cinquino and Robin Michaelson, I thank you for your creative suggestions for making our book reader-friendly. And as always, a special thank you to my agent, Pierre Lehu, who encouraged my relationship with Rodale.

The names of some of the schools, administrators, students, and other individuals who contributed so much to this book are listed below. Many more schools and individuals who assisted with the survey and study preferred to remain anonymous. If there are any others that slipped my attention and were missed, I thank you all.

Thank you to my adult interviewees who shared stories of their childhood overweight problems and successes: Denise Foley, Jocelyn Franciose, Sandra Furton Gabriel, Christina Gaugler, Cindy Gittleman, Caryl Greenberg, Kathy Holecek, Tammy Janke, Diane Lind, Niki Lisk, Rhonda Malas, Jodi Marcou, Margaret McClung, Patricia M. Merrifield, Pat Nystrom, Mark S. Sherman, and Anita Thompkins.

Appreciation is extended to the administrators and other individuals who helped enlist the participation of schools and students in the survey: Cheré Beavers, Barbara Bennett, Sandi Bisceglia, Mark Bregar, Francine Butzine, Ruth Carlstrom, William Christ, Lisa Christensen, Jeri Cocannouer, Reno DiOreo, Judy Freeman, Joanne Haddad, Gail P. Hammond, Betsy Hays, Pat Hollingsworth, Susan Jones, Nyle Kardatzke, Howard Kelly, Candice Konicki, Chris Kraay, Roxanne Lopatin, Vivian Lopatin, Joel Orleck, Marianne Richardson, Janet Rimm, Dr. Julia Roberts, Susan Savolainen, Brenda Sherman, Frances Sherman, Lynn Sherman, Joan Franklin Smutny, Carol Van Straten, Lori Wehr, and Pamela Wells.

Thank you to the following students who assisted me in the study. There were many others, but it was difficult to gather parent permissions for use of their names: Rachael Hauptly, Erin Koszalinski, Ben Madsen, Scott Merrifield, Daniel Rimm, Hannah Rimm, Rachel Rimm, Vic Scheller, Jonathan Van Geffen, and Amber Young.

School participation for my survey was absolutely necessary and involved commitment from teachers, administrators, and middle school students. Thanks so much to the following schools and others that preferred privacy for their part in the study: Atkins Public Schools, Atkins, AR; C. A. Frost K-8 School, Grand Rapids, MI; Center for Gifted, National-Louis University, and Quest Academy, Palatine, IL; The Center for Gifted Studies, Western Kentucky University, Bowling Green, KY; Chandler Junior High School, Chandler, OK; DeLong Middle School, Eau Claire, WI; Girl Scouts of Genesee Valley Inc., Rochester, NY; Hathaway Brown School, Shaker Heights, OH; The Heritage School, Newnan, GA; Hopkins Elementary School, Mentor, OH; Lehigh Valley Summerbridge, Bethlehem, PA; The

Linsly School, Wheeling, WV; Meigs Magnet Middle School, Nashville, TN; North Middle School, Great Falls, MT; North Star School, Eau Claire, WI; Parkside Intermediate School, Westlake, OH; Plantation Key School, Tavernier, FL; St. Henry School, Watertown, WI; St. Mary of the Assumption School, Mentor, OH; School District of Shiocton, Shiocton, WI; Sherwood Park K-8 School, Grand Rapids, MI; South Middle School, Eau Claire, WI; Sycamore School, Indianapolis, IN; University School, Shaker Heights, OH; University School at the University of Tulsa, Tulsa, OK; Vilonia Elementary School, Vilonia, AR; and West Elementary School, Great Falls, MT.

Other students and adults who participated in the survey, focus groups, or interviews were from the following additional cities: Allentown, PA; Appleton, WI; Boiling Springs, PA; Brandon, MS; Branford, CT; Brookline, MA; Cleveland, OH; Cleveland Heights, OH; Colorado Springs, CO; Corvallis, MT; East Brunswick, NJ; Eastchester, NJ; Evanston, IL; Macungie, PA; Milwaukee, WI; Ridgewood, NJ; Rocky River, OH; St. Paul, MN; San Antonio, TX; and Wescosville, PA.

INTRODUCTION

Overweight children are too often the outcasts, lepers, and untouchables in our middle and high schools. They may be shunned by their peers, stereotyped as dumb and lazy, rejected for friendship and scholarship, and left to wither on the vine and nurse their sorrows with sweets that perpetuate their problems. The world does not seem to understand, care about, empathize with, or even wish to reach out and help them. Every day, the numbers of overweight children are increasing dramatically. These children desperately require emotional rescue.

My groundbreaking findings about the emotional lives of overweight children arrived by serendipity. In order to advise parents in a book about the differences between their own middle school years and those of their children, I surveyed more than 5,400 middle schoolers, ages 7 through 14. At the moment, that book remains on hold because the survey's unexpected findings about children who perceived themselves as overweight were so gripping and disturbing. As a psychologist who works with children and adolescents and as a parent, I understand and empathize with the incredible sorrows these children feel. I know directly from their parents, their teachers, and their own sad voices the psychological abuses they suffer. But even I was astonished at the depth of these children's suffering and how their weight affects nearly every aspect of their lives. The more I found out about them, the more I felt compelled to assemble my data regarding the emotional impact of overweight to broadcast to parents and professionals the extraordinarily distressing dilemma facing overweight children. Not only does public health data tell us that these children are destined for un-healthy, foreshortened lives, but their childhood experience is steeped in such bigotry that the options for reversing their diminished station in life are few without our active involvement. This book is a call to adults who intentionally or unintentionally perpetuate the merciless bias to instead un-derstand and help our overweight kids.

My four-page research survey was filled out by students in grades three through eight who lived in 18 different states and were from small and large, public and parochial, independent, urban, suburban, and rural schools. (While the survey has broad representation, it cannot be construed as a random sample. It was impossible to select schools at random because it is difficult to enlist schools' participation in any surveys. The schools that I was able to enlist did me a great favor, and I appreciate their contribution to my research.) The survey the schools gave students included 36 questions about children's descriptions of their characteristics, worries and fears, family relationships, peer relations, interests, activities, and self-confidence. One question asked children to describe whether they were very over-weight, somewhat overweight, average weight, somewhat underweight, or very underweight.

Two percent of the children who reported their weight, or 113 children, described themselves as very overweight, and another 17 percent, or 908 children, described themselves as somewhat overweight. Fifty-nine percent (3,092) considered themselves average weight, 18 percent (944) somewhat underweight, and 4 percent (200) very underweight. Percentages were al-most identical for girls and boys. The percentages in each weight category from my sample differed somewhat from the prevalence findings on over-weight announced by researchers Cynthia L. Ogden, Ph.D., and colleagues in the *Journal of the American Medical Association*. Ogden is an epidemi-ologist at the National Center for Health Statistics Centers for Disease Con-trol and Prevention. Recent research (1999–2000) found 15.3 percent of today's children to be overweight. Because we don't know exact weights of the children in my sample, we can't determine the children's actual weight category based on standard medical evaluations. However, if we match those who perceived themselves as either very overweight or somewhat overweight (19 percent in total), my sample showed a higher percentage of overweight children. (The fact of the matter is that young children rarely know their actual weights, so asking that question would not have yielded usable information.)

However, the validity of the findings is quite solid, as evidenced by its consistent pattern. For if the children's descriptions of their weight had been substantially wrong—that is, if thin children considered themselves overweight or overweight children described themselves as average—the uniqueness in responses of these groups of children would not have been so vivid in such a wide number and variety of categories. That is to say, gross inaccuracies in children's estimates of their weight would have destroyed the trends that were so obvious, and they would have erased the statistically significant differences that were inescapably present. For example, consider a finding I describe in more detail in chapter 5 about children's activities. As you would expect, children who described themselves as very overweight and somewhat overweight reported spending more time in passive activities, like television and computers, and less time in sports than average-weight children. If these children had described themselves as overweight but were actually average or thin, there would have been fewer or no differences between the overweight and average-weight kids for such variables as television and sports. The coherent patterns of the findings of the study substantiate the reasonable accuracy of the children's self-descriptions of their weight.

Keep in mind that the critical conclusions in my study aren't so much to establish the exact number of children with weight problems but to take the first-ever look at what these kids are going through. What overweight kids said about themselves was so startling and descriptive that it reveals the shocking distress that overweight children experience. Their emotional distress, a clear call for help, initiated my further study of overweight children.

I recall the exact moment when I recognized the dramatic impact of children's descriptions of their overweight on their worries. I was visiting my son, Eric Rimm, Sc.D., who, as a nutritional epidemiologist at Harvard University, studies how diet and lifestyle factors affect health. I was looking at my survey results, which included the analysis of worries by each weight group, when I muttered, almost to myself but within Eric's hearing: "These poor fat children. They have so many worries, they hardly have a chance." Eric's off-the-cuff response was "Well, they should worry. We're having an epidemic of obesity. We'll have a huge public health problem if they don't do something about their weight." As we sat down to eat our breakfast together and he shared with me the new public health research that worried him, my anxiety about these poor children only grew. Not only was I concerned about the public health consequences, I was also frustrated that my epidemiologist son, along with the rest of the world, would not understand the emotional trauma these children were experiencing that prevented them from doing anything to help their weight problems. I knew from my clinical work as a psychologist that children under such peer, school, and family pressures would turn either to food for consolation or to bulimia or anorexia in desperation. Both are emotionally and physically destructive.

As the media began broadcasting the depressing statistics about increasing obesity, I felt compelled to convince my publisher that my unique survey could be used to provide insight to parents, counselors, and educators so they could join me in a rescue mission for these misunderstood children. Indeed, we discovered no other book that uncovered the psychological trauma that these overweight children were experiencing. If we could mobilize caring adults to understand the emotional impact of overweight, we could surely prevent emotional disaster for children as well as intervene in this public health epidemic.

In addition to the quantitative survey, I conducted focus groups with more than 300 children from four different cities. In our conversations, I specifically asked the children to discuss their attitudes toward their overweight peers. I also talked with at least a dozen overweight young people, with parents and teachers of overweight children, and with families that came to me for clinical help. Finally, I interviewed 20 adults who had been overweight in childhood and who, for the most part, had coped with their weight problems successfully and thus were models for healthy lifestyles. And since my son Eric's experience in nutritional epidemiology is so broad and in-depth, I asked him to share his knowledge of the immense public health problem. He has written an important chapter for our book, chapter 2, that describes this national emergency. The other chapters of the book both describe my findings and research conclusions and offer prescriptive advice for adults to help solve the problems of overweight children from the inside out.

There are references in our book to the research in my book *See Jane Win*, so you may want some background on that study. My daughters, Sara Rimm-Kaufman, Ph.D., and Ilonna Rimm, M.D., Ph.D., assisted me in an extensive survey related to the childhoods of more than 1,000 successful women. That research was hailed by Oprah Winfrey and Katie Couric as groundbreaking, and *See Jane Win* became a *New York Times* best seller for 2 months, in July and August 2000. Its findings about high achievement provide a road map for parenting girls toward success, but its findings also cast worries about the success of children whose overweight makes them less likely to be motivated and confident in their intelligence.

It is my intense hope that this composite of quantitative and qualitative information will inspire parents, teachers, counselors, pediatricians, and others to care about and understand overweight children and to guide them toward healthier lifestyles. Our book is written for adults who are involved with children of all ages, from preschool to middle and high schools. While the survey and interviews showed that children's awareness of their overweight often surfaced during the middle school years, patterns of isolation and contempt for overweight children begin early and continue to adulthood.

It is equally important that these findings assist in eradicating the ugly stereotypes that prevent overweight kids of all ages from emerging from a quagmire of prejudice and drive them toward overeating. Rescuing these children can give them hope that they may live up to their potential and make significant contributions to society. Rescuing these children can also stem the serious national epidemic of obesity that has grave consequences for future health problems. If you have children in your family who are overweight or you work with such children in schools or clinics, our book is for you. It will provide the rescue strategies you've searched for to help guide your children to heal themselves.

CHAPTER 1

THE URGENCY FOR OVERWEIGHT CHILDREN:
The Trauma Our Children Experience

It's incredible to realize that the percentage of children who are obese has tripled in the past 30 years, creating a national epidemic that will likely have dire public health consequences for our country. While overweight children may hear only a collective chorus of "You must diet" and "You have to exercise," the answer to reducing obesity is to understand what our children are going through. Hear their voices as they plead for help.

"No One Knows about My Sadness"

I'm the clown in my crowd and I can keep kids laughing hilariously. I try to hold on to friends that way. When I play basketball or touch football on the playground, I try to keep up, but I'm huffing and puffing, and other guys aren't even tired. I'm slow and last at everything, and I'm definitely the last guy kids pick for the team. I still laugh and joke at school, though, so everyone thinks I'm well-adjusted. No one knows about my sadness. I finally broke down and told my mom how left-out and different I feel. Can any kid be this lonely and keep joking?

Andrew, seventh grade

"I Don't Exist"

The popular kids scorn me because they see me as unfit to talk to. I try to say hi, and they don't recognize my existence in the universe. I don't exist. They ignore me, or sometimes they call me a fag. My old friend won't talk to me anymore. He's become popular, and being friends with me threatens his popularity. High school won't be much better because there will be the sports jocks, and they'll be even more homophobic and make me seem like even more of a nerd. I'm not looking forward to it.

Matt, eighth grade

The emotional trauma for overweight and obese children is far beyond what most families realize. One recent study showed just how bad overweight children feel about themselves. During a 6-month period in 2002, 106 children and adolescents were referred to an academic children's hospital to be evaluated for obesity. When these obese children and adolescents completed a quality-of-life survey, their scores not only were significantly lower than those of normal-weight adolescents but were as low as children receiving chemotherapy for cancer.

And they often feel so bad about themselves because society feels so bad about them. Bigotry toward children who are overweight is perhaps the last unexplored and ignored prejudice. Children and adults alike almost seem to relish the nasty remarks and sarcasm directed at fat children, sometimes even if the taunters themselves are overweight. They don't seem to feel guilty when making the offensive comments, almost as if they believe they have a right to punish children who are overweight. Or else adults mistakenly believe that sarcastic comments will encourage children to lose weight, but the psychological impact of that savagery typically provokes these children to eat even more and exercise less.

Unfortunately, children become overweight when their genetics and environment lead them to eat too much and exercise too little. Being overweight negatively affects almost every aspect of their psychological profile:

their self-esteem, friendships, confidence in their intelligence, physical development, family relationships, and hopes for their future. Most of all, it dramatically affects their long-term physical and mental health.

Our book provides readers with insight on the emotional issues that perpetuate the problems overweight children of all ages experience, as well as the knowledge necessary to rescue these children from emotional disaster. Our advice is directed toward parents and professionals so they can empathize with overweight children to create an alliance to assist them in developing healthier, more balanced adolescent and adult lives.

The many emotions associated with both food and exercise make helping a child more complex.

THE EMOTIONS OF FOOD

It's important that you consider the emotional attributes of eating—some of which we've been conditioned to feel since infancy—to understand all the dynamics that can come into play in our households.

Food Is Love

From the moment we hold our newborn infants in our arms while nursing them, our babies are conditioned to equate food with love. When a baby cries, food is the first comfort we provide. Even as he toddles and walks, we think that a sad, cranky child is a hungry child. We pacify a crying, complaining child with crackers, cereal, juice, or milk, guessing that his tears communicate hunger so if we feed him, he will smile or sleep peacefully. If food is love, then the withdrawal of food is the withdrawal of love.

Food Is Health

A baby's chubby legs, her sweet, round face, and that delicious double chin convince us that she's healthy. Her fat little belly, flabby arms, and pudgy cheeks assure you you've fed your baby well. We believe fat babies are healthy babies. "Eat, my child, and grow healthy and strong" translates into any language and through all cultures. We adore our pudgy little babies and feel gratified that they are pictures of health. If fat babies prove we're successful parents, how can we risk serving our children less food and continue to trust that they're healthy?

Food Is Celebration

Every birthday, every holiday, and even good report cards are celebrated with family feasts. Confirmations, bar mitzvahs, graduations, and weddings (think *My Big Fat Greek Wedding!*) are crowned with elaborate food preparations and marvelous-tasting food. Family and friend relationships at every age are immersed in food. The more special the occasion, the more likely the food will be excessive, fattening, and unhealthy. Because we are so conditioned to celebrating with food, it seems inappropriate and uncomfortable to celebrate with less food, or even less elaborate and less fattening foods.

Food Is Basic

Even if we aren't celebrating or proclaiming our love, we love to eat. Food does more than appease our hunger. It pleases our palates, and we delight in its taste. Even as little babies eat their first pabulum, they make "yummy" sounds. We salivate at the smell of fresh-baked pizza, yearn for thick milk shakes, and crave chocolate. Doesn't it always seem like the most fattening foods are the most irresistible? Food is a necessity; we can't do without it. Thus, too much food and unhealthy, delicious foods will always be there to tempt us.

Food Is Social Status

Important job interviews are often conducted at elegant restaurants. Significant agreements are sealed with posh dinners. Government visitors are welcomed with exquisite banquets. Gourmet refreshments signify the power, status, and wealth of the host. The number of stars awarded to a restaurant dictates not only a restaurant's standing but also the social status of the clientele it attracts. People are motivated to eat elaborately to show off their success, but eating elaborately rarely means eating healthfully and almost always means eating immoderately. Although young children usually eat the same fried chicken fingers and french fries they have at fast-food places even when taken to fancy bistros, they learn early from their parents that these restaurants are somehow better. By the teen years, when their dates take them for pizza or burgers in a high-status restaurant, they believe those girlfriends or boyfriends are "cool." Before proms, the popular kids select the best restaurants, signifying their social success among their peers.

Food Is Power

One parent may lead a clean-your-plate club, while the other parent may lead a don't-eat-so-much club. Often you can add a grandparent who may advocate for a let-the-poor-hungry-child-have-dessert club. Hence, arguments ensue. Children quickly learn that food provides them with power. To eat or not to eat can affect how adults relate to each other or how they treat their children at mealtime or snack time. Tempers flare just because Elizabeth refuses to eat her beans, or hostilities ensue when Roger wants a second Popsicle. Some children direct the dinner table with their adamant refusal to eat anything or their insistence on eating too much. They control whether parents are angry at each other or act respectfully to grandparents, or they influence whether their sisters or brothers attract more attention than they, all by eating or not eating. Thus, children may become empowered as little dictators by using food to manipulate their parents. "Love is a battlefield," to quote a popular song lyric; the same can be said for food.

Food Can Become a Problem

Regular visits to the family physician typically celebrate weight gain. "He's doing so nicely" and "She's gaining well" confirm our own assessment of our healthy children. Pediatricians compare children's weights and heights against a standard growth chart, and parents display pride for children who are at the highest percentiles. When the chubbiness of infancy doesn't disappear, we refer to our toddler or preschooler as "a little chunky," "pudgy," or "on the heavy side" in a flattering way, but we can't help but begin to notice the plumpness. We try not to talk about it, deny there's any weight problem, and continue to be thankful for our healthy child until our annual doctor's visit elicits a response we've unconsciously begun to worry about—"Your son is getting to be too heavy" or "Your child is off the charts"—and suddenly we feel urgent and threatening emotions.

We remember that Aunt LaKeisha or Uncle Gerald was overweight, or, worse yet, we've struggled with our own weight problems. We say to ourselves that our children are going to have "the same struggle as I did" or "problems like Grandma had." We feel guilty by genetic implication, yet continue to call our children "chubby," "chunky," "fleshy," "a little big," "hefty," even "roly-poly," but carefully avoid the word "fat." And we certainly don't classify them as "obese." *Maybe she'll outgrow it,* we hope to ourselves, or *I'd better watch what he eats,* or *Should I hide the cookies?* Anger or sadness stirs within us as we recall our own childhood or that of another overweight family member.

And at some point, and sometimes quite suddenly, everything changes. Once we become convinced that our children are overweight, all the wonderful emotional attributes of food suddenly cause incredible problems for them and for us. Now there are calories to worry about. We feel compelled to tell our overweight children they're eating too much or too often. We'll want to give them smaller servings of birthday cake and ice cream, and cut down on the fries and chips. We can no longer encourage them by saying, "Eat, my child, and you'll be healthy." Instead, we're forced to change our roles from giving food to withdrawing or limiting food. What mixed feelings we have! As parents we must now restrain ourselves from giving food, and, worse yet, we must deprive our children of the joy of eating. Sometimes it feels as if we are depriving our children of love.

As we hide the cookies and candy, we reduce our love relationship to a power struggle. Celebrations become battlegrounds instead of happy times. The yummy tastes of food are clouded by guilt and calorie counting. Our fat children watch brothers, sisters, and friends enjoy food they can't or shouldn't have. They feel cheated, deprived, and rejected and nourish their sad feelings with more food—which is tied to love, after all. The power that children wield, by eating or not eating, becomes an instrument of their control. Children manipulate adults even more as their overweight causes them to feel powerless in a peer society that is destructive and obnoxious toward overweight children. The food that brings such joy, health, pleasure, love, and celebration to most people now begins to spell disaster for overweight children.

THE EMOTIONS OF EXERCISE

As we think about how to resolve our children's eating habits, we also wonder how to encourage more activity since an important component of weight loss is exercise. Yet exercise, like food, is also fraught with emotion.

Physical Activity As a Lifestyle

Our babies crawl, toddle, walk, and run. We marvel as their skills develop. We compliment their coordination. But what if our children are heavy and awkward? We notice them fall, struggle, sit, watch TV, play computer games, draw, read, do puzzles, and immerse themselves in lethargic inactivity. Couch potatoes, mouse potatoes, and bookworms don't burn calories. Television viewing, Web browsing, and reading provide a fountain of information, but they don't use energy.

All of the above are lifestyle choices that can coexist with an active lifestyle or replace physical activity. And these lifestyle patterns begin in childhood. So why, we ask ourselves, does average-weight Deirdre love to run, dance, and play, while her overweight sister Denise simply sits, sulks, or slumbers? Deirdre wants us to join her on a bike ride, but Denise needs to be convinced, persuaded, and even threatened to get her butt onto a bicycle seat. What can we do about Denise's inactivity?

Feeling Awkward

Many heavy children are surprisingly graceful, but clumsy, klutzy, and awkward best describe the physical coordination of some overweight children. After all, they need to coordinate a larger body. How can we expect her to dance with the ballerinas or flip with the gymnasts? How do we expect him to bat with the ball team or skate with the hockey enthusiasts? It's embarrassing. We cringe when they're up at bat and flush with embarrassment when they're center stage. We can't praise their performance, or when we do, our praise is not believable. Soon they know they lack grace and skill. Why wouldn't they prefer reading, art, or television? When we urge physical activity, they protest, make excuses, and argue. We decide ultimately we have different battles to fight. We feel sorry for them, and they sense our sadness, which makes them feel even less adequate. They sulk and escape back to television, books, art, or computers. They avoid physical activity, and although we know they should stay active, we are relieved from the embarrassment their awkward participation has made us feel.

RESCUING YOUR OVERWEIGHT CHILD

When a family struggles with raising an overweight child or children, they feel alone with their problem. When children wage war against obesity, they feel isolated, cheated, and overwhelmed. Confronting this serious problem *alone* dooms families and kids to failure and obesity, in light of the emotional context of food and exercise I've described. We're here to help.

However, please don't expect this book to be a diet or exercise guide for your child. Our goal is to help you protect your child's emotional life while you are searching for the right eating and exercise plan to correct your child's condition. What's more, chances are that whatever lifestyle and diet changes you make in your family, they will not be effective unless you cope with the emotional crisis your child may be experiencing. With that in mind, the remainder of our book will help you understand your child's psychological needs. As you learn to address these needs, you can better focus on choosing your favorite recipes and activities to go along with your child's emotional health plan.

Chapters 3 through 7 guide you on the path to helping children of all ages. Each chapter has two parts. The first part includes my research findings, including survey results, interviews, focus groups, and other research related to the different facets of your child's emotional life. The second part of each chapter describes the rescue techniques—the practical approaches—that parents and professionals can apply to help overweight children.

Overweight children do require help from adults, but our suggestions are designed to help adults teach overweight children to rescue themselves. Children must ultimately learn to rescue themselves both from the psychological abuse that is directed toward them and from unhealthy obesity. Because overweight attracts psychological abuse, and the abuse in turn worsens the weight problem, rescue plans must target healthy lifestyles that maintain reasonable weight, protect children from abuse, and deal with the continual learning, developmental, and family issues crucial to children's self-actualization. The goal of our rescue operation is to destroy the disadvantages that overweight children struggle with and to level the health, psychological, and educational playing fields for all children, whatever their weights.

Each chapter targets a special issue that affects overweight children, though in real life these issues overlap. Chapter 3 describes how children's overweight affects their social and emotional adjustment, particularly their self-confidence, self-descriptions, and attitudes toward their peers. Included are ways to raise self-esteem and improve social confidence.

Chapter 4 focuses on the unexpected impact on the academic confidence and achievement of overweight compared with average-weight children. You'll also find strategies for inspiring academic confidence and reversing underachievement.

Chapter 5 compares the interests and activities of overweight children with those of average-weight children. It also explains the psychological pain overweight children experience from their involvement in the very activities that can help them lose weight. The chapter offers advice on energizing children toward physical activities.

Chapter 6 discusses the developmental and sexual maturity issues that increase problems for heavy children and helps parents guide children in coping with these.

Chapter 7 details some problematic family scenarios that actually foster overweight in children and shows you how you can change those.

Chapter 8 summarizes the strategies and prioritizes the step-by-step solutions for rescuing the emotional lives of overweight children who are on the heavy side of a great divide.

The epilogue concludes the book with the importance of teaching overweight children to optimistically look toward their future. There is hope for overweight children, as you can see from Alyssa's story. Her teacher asked her to write about herself, and she did.

"I Have New Hope for My Future"

Ever since I was a little kid, I was fat, and that made me feel different from other kids. Kids left me out of their groups. I had absolutely no one to play with on the playground; not a single friend. On Valentine's Day, when other kids got valentines saying "I love you" or "Be mine," my valentine had an elephant on it. Some love! I felt like an elephant. A wall kept going up, higher and higher, separating me from everyone. I felt imprisoned until this year. This year my teacher liked me. She helped me find my talents. She told me I was good at writing, math, and music and that I had a good personality. Her confidence in me made me feel different, but in a good way. I started making friends and felt smart and better about myself. Now I think the wall is tumbling down, and I have new hope for my future.

Alyssa, eighth grade

Whether you're a parent, counselor, or teacher, you can help to pull down your children's walls of confinement just as Alyssa's teacher helped her. The solutions in our book are based on effective strategies of healthy parenting and counseling that have worked for overweight children in the real world, as proven by the adult success stories and my own private practice of working with all kinds of children. The rescue techniques can help you to guide your own children to physical and emotional good health and toward a brighter future.

Before we examine the emotional lives of our overweight children, my son, Eric Rimm, Sc.D., will describe the magnitude and the urgency of this public health problem. The alarming statistics in the next chapter will only increase if we cannot rescue these children from obesity's terrible grip.

CHAPTER 2

HEAVY KIDS, HEAVY HEARTS:
The Public Health Implications of Obesity

How many times in the past week, month, or year have you read a newspaper headline or seen a television news story about the growing problem of obesity? Probably quite a few times, since the grim news of this public health problem is ever present. There is no doubt that obesity is at epidemic levels in almost all age and ethnic groups in America, yet we still have not been able to stop or even slow the rise in obesity rates. This is why I have dedicated much of my professional life to the study of this epidemic and the related health conditions that result from being overweight.

I'm pleased to be writing this chapter for my mother's examination of the emotional effects of overweight on children. This dovetails with my work as a nutritional epidemiologist on the faculty at the Harvard School of Public Health for the past 11 years. Although you might think of an epidemiologist as someone who works at the Centers for Disease Control and Prevention (CDC) in Atlanta and fights the spread of infectious diseases like AIDS, SARS, and the Ebola virus, many more epidemiologists in the United States work to understand the causes of chronic conditions like diabetes, cancer, heart disease, and obesity. At Harvard, I focus on associations between diet and lifestyle factors as they relate to the risks of obesity and heart disease—two major disease burdens in our society. My job as a researcher is to measure and document the problem, study its causes, and, in the case of obesity, find out how it will affect the occurrence, or incidence, of future disease.

For obesity, epidemiologists historically studied the occurrence only among adults, but now much more focus has been placed on the growing problem in children. Because if we can't help children from becoming overweight, how will we help or prevent them from becoming overweight as adults?

In this chapter, you will begin to understand the extent of the obesity problem among children in the United States and gain insights into its root causes. It's important to know the statistics and figures in order to comprehend the magnitude of this epidemic; for example, do you realize that obesity is estimated to be associated with over $90 billion in health care costs per year in the United States?

But the true health burden can best be understood by looking at the long-term medical ramifications of childhood obesity. As extensive research on the health effects of obesity among adults has shown (as described in a recent review in the *New England Journal of Medicine*), excess body weight among adult men and women leads to a greater risk of heart disease, cancer, diabetes, hypertension, stroke, and gallbladder disease, as well as other severe health conditions.

Researchers are beginning to look more in-depth at the short- and long-term health consequences of obesity among children, and I'll describe some of the more recent findings. However, most research does not capture the emotional consequences of childhood obesity that subsequent chapters of this book will describe.

WHAT IS OBESITY?

In simple terms, obesity is an imbalance between energy consumed and energy burned. Thus, the root cause of obesity in children is likely a combination of too much energy—calories—consumed and too little energy expended on physical activity.

Of course, an individual's weight does fluctuate over time as small changes in activity or diet can lead to big changes in weight if the changes are sustained over a long period of time.

To illustrate, let's consider two seventh-grade girls with similar builds but different eating and exercise patterns: Molly and Susan, both of whom are 5 feet 1 inch tall and weigh 100 pounds. Each exercises once a week for an hour during gym class. Molly also plays on a soccer team for 3 hours a week 6 months of the year (2 hours of practice and an hour of match play). To sustain a healthy weight and to provide enough energy to play soccer, Molly needs to eat more calories than Susan, who watches television for the same 3 hours that Molly runs on the soccer field.

If Molly decided to give up soccer but maintain the same diet, she would gain approximately 7 pounds by year's end. If Susan joined Molly on the soccer field, she could lose the equivalent amount of weight or more, depending on her diet.

Without a change in diet or exercise pattern, what would happen if either student decided to drink an extra 12-ounce can of regular cola every day? If either consumed this extra 145 calories every day without compensating with extra exercise or removing something else from her diet, she would gain an estimated 12 to 15 pounds in 1 year. All that weight just from one can of cola a day! (This shows how quickly the super-sized drinks at fast-food restaurants could affect the obesity problem among children.)

These numbers are estimates and may differ from child to child because a child's body is very efficient at compensating for varying energy demands. However, I included these hypothetical examples to illustrate the importance of the effects of even small changes in diet or exercise on body weight.

DEFINING OBESITY

There are some highly sophisticated methods for assessing obesity through measuring true fat mass in children and adults, but most are very expensive or time-consuming and cannot be used easily in a home, doctor's office, or school setting. Thankfully, there are basic measures that allow a doctor, a school health aide, or even a parent to determine if a child is much heavier than is normal.

The simplest and most obvious measure is body weight, which can be quickly and easily assessed by a child, parent, pediatrician, or school nurse. However, because of height differences, weight alone is not always the best marker of obesity. Obviously, because of the difference in absolute weight due to lean body mass (your bones, muscles, and body organs), somebody 6 feet 4 inches tall should weigh more than somebody 5 feet 2 inches tall.

To account for these differences, the body mass index, or BMI, was developed. Since the BMI—calculated as weight in kilograms (kg) divided by the square of height in meters (m)—takes into consideration both weight and body size, this standardized measure can be compared across individuals regardless of body height. BMI has been found, in detailed clinical studies, to be most closely related to actual body density, or fat mass. This just means that a short person and a tall person with a BMI of 25 kg/m^2 (the cutoff for being overweight) will have equal amounts of fat relative to their heights.

If you want to calculate your own BMI, convert your weight (1 pound = 0.455 kilogram) and height (1 inch = 0.0254 meter) to metric units and calculate weight/height^2—or you can find detailed charts and BMI calculators online or at your doctor's office. In general a BMI of less than 25 kg/m^2 is normal weight, 25 to 29.9 kg/m^2 is overweight, and 30-plus kg/m^2 is obese.

For children, body mass index is also frequently used for research and clinical purposes. However, the cutoffs of 25 and 30 kg/m^2 used among adults to define overweight and obesity are not as appropriate for children until they attain their maximum height. The most accepted cutoff for the clinical diagnosis of overweight among children is a BMI at or above the 95th percentile for children of the same age and sex. The percentiles for BMI have been developed from growth charts from national surveys conducted over the past 30 years in the United States.

For example, a 10-year-old girl is overweight if she has a BMI of 23 kg/m^2, but because a 16-year-old girl has matured further, she is not considered overweight until she reaches a BMI of 29 kg/m^2. A cutoff of the

85th percentile is frequently used as the "at risk for overweight" category. If you want more detail, check out www.cdc.gov/growthcharts, where the CDC has growth charts for all ages. Your pediatrician also can help you determine your child's percentile. (Please note that for children under 2 years old, weight for length is used as a better guide for determining overweight.)

HOW BAD IS THE OBESITY EPIDEMIC?

Now that you have a better understanding of the simple tools epidemiologists use to measure and define obesity, I want to paint a picture of the obesity epidemic. The most recent data available from a nationally representative survey found that a whopping 64.5 percent of the U.S. population was overweight (30.5 percent of the population was obese). That's right, nearly two out of every three Americans are overweight!

What is even more astonishing is how fast the rates of obesity have risen. Only 6 to 10 years ago, only 55.9 percent of the population was overweight (22.9 percent obese). No other disease or health condition even comes close to being so widespread across America. This is why epidemiologists consider obesity a true public health epidemic.

Even more revealing is the incidence of obesity by state. For the past 15 years or so, the CDC has estimated, on a yearly basis, the percentage of the population in each state that is obese (remember, that is a BMI greater than 30 kg/m^2).

In 1990, in 33 states 10 to 14 percent of the population was obese; the rest of the states had lower percentages. Five years later, only in 22 states was 10 to 14 percent of the population obese; in 28 other states, the obese population was now 15 to 19 percent. By decade's end, only one state had an obesity rate as low as 10 to 14 percent. In the most recent available update (released in 2003, for rates until 2001), 20 states had rates of 15 to 19 percent obesity, 28 states had rates of 20 to 24 percent obesity, and one state (Mississippi) had an obesity rate of more than 25 percent. These increases in obesity rates are staggering in their magnitude as well as their implication for the future health of our nation.

Not surprisingly, the growing rise in obesity among adults is mirrored in a similar climb in obesity among children. In the most recent analysis of time trends of childhood obesity over the past 30 years, CDC researchers described stunning increases in obesity in a relatively short time period. During the 1960s and early 1970s, only small changes were reported; at that time, approximately 5 percent of children were above the 95th percentile for BMI. (This is not surprising since, by definition, once a cutoff is determined for the 95th percentile, 5 percent of all children will naturally be above this threshold and be considered overweight.) However, when researchers used the same cutoff to define obesity in children in the 1980s through the year 2000, there was a dramatic increase in the prevalence of obesity (see figure 2.1 on page 22).

For example, between 1976 and 1980 approximately 6.4 percent of girls 6 to 11 years of age were overweight, slightly higher than the 5 percent expected. However, by 2000, 14.5 percent of girls in the same age range were overweight in the United States.

Obesity has grown equally quickly among boys. For example, 5.3 percent of 12- to 19-year-old boys were overweight between 1976 and 1980; this had tripled to 15.5 percent by 2000. These incredible increases show what a problem obesity has become in just the past 2 decades. And the end result is that we have an epidemic of obesity in all age groups.

HOW DO CHILDREN BECOME OVERWEIGHT?

While obesity has a modest genetic component, this dramatic increase in obesity in only 20 years in children and adults suggests a strong environmental influence because certainly our genetic makeup has not evolved that quickly. What does this mean for parents and children? If a parent is overweight, it should not be assumed that the child, too, will be overweight. If

Figure 2.1
Trends in Overweight for Children
Birth through 19 Years, by Sex and Age Group

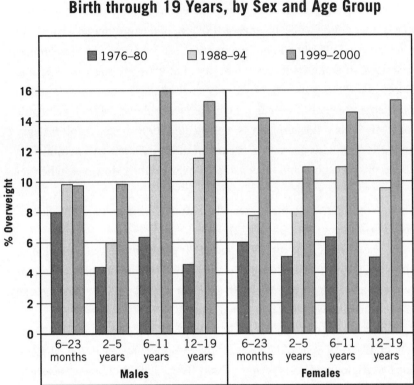

Reprinted from Ogden, L.L. et al. (2002). Prevalence and trends in overweight among US children and adolescents, 1999–2000. *Journal of the American Medical Association* 288 (14) : 1728–1732.

both parent and child can change their diet and exercise habits together, they can overcome the effect of genetics on body weight.

So how do children become overweight? This simple question has been raised and discussed endlessly by pediatricians, researchers, public health commissioners, school board superintendents, teachers, parents, and many other concerned professionals who have seen the disturbing rise in obesity in the United States.

Some hypothesize that the increase in television watching and the related drop in physical activity has led to a society of sedentary parents and sedentary kids. Unfortunately, the amount of time we all sit in front of a desk, television, computer screen, or video game continues to rise. Do you realize that in 2000, the average child watched television an alarming 3.5 hours per day? Of all the data in this chapter, this fact surprised me the most. However, when I reflected on my busy schedule and my family's, I realized that without a conscious effort to plan alternative activities and encourage and participate in my children's hobbies, reading, and school functions, it would be very easy to allow my kids to plop down in front of the television while I caught up on house chores, work, and exercise. So instead, my wife and I have set TV-watching limits for our children, and we guard against using television as a reward for good behavior. (See chapter 5 for more on this.)

Reliable research data suggests that while you watch television, your body's metabolic rate—the speed at which it burns calories—is even slower than the resting metabolic rate, which reflects the basic caloric needs of an individual when at rest but sitting and quietly reading. Thus, television watching may be considered an "extreme" sedentary activity that, when repeated over and over every day, leads to fewer calories burned and a steady climb in body weight. Besides putting children in a trance, television shows and ads also barrage them with commercial messages to buy more high-calorie, nutrient-empty foods. While television alone will not create a world of overweight child zombies, every successive generation seems to have become even more dependent on television as a major (and largely negative) influence in their young lives.

I realize that many people use television as a way to relax and escape from daily worries. But in order to protect your family from becoming part of the disturbing trends we're seeing, you may want to find other ways of relaxing: perhaps simply resting in a comfy easy chair in a quiet room— without the television on. Or, as an alternative, use your time in front of the television more efficiently. In the winter I watch my favorite sports shows while burning calories on my exercise bike. Exercising in front of the television works for me and has conveyed the importance of physical activity to my children. My daughter bikes with me on a small recumbent bike, and my young son participates, too, by lifting 2-pound weights. I don't think the

HEALTH CONSEQUENCES OF CHILDHOOD OBESITY

The pernicious onset of obesity can cause a lifetime of adverse health conditions. Here we list several examples of health problems that have been associated with childhood obesity. In many cases, such as low self-esteem or diminished quality of life, obesity can impact children in their preteens or teens, whereas with other examples, such as eye disease or cancer, childhood obesity may predispose a person to earlier onset of these diseases as an adult.

- Young adult eating disorders
- Psychosocial ailments
- Reduced quality of life
- Low self-esteem
- Depression
- Early age of puberty
- Infertility
- Asthma

- Eye disorders
- Sleep apnea or sleep disorders
- Diabetes
- High blood pressure
- Heart disease
- Cancer
- Gallbladder disease
- Stroke

weights will help him too much, but at 3 years old, he already understands the importance of exercise. And when we are all watching television together, I'll sneak in a few skeptical criticisms about food commercials when my kids are staring longingly at some "food product" that's being billed as a healthy choice by a fast-food restaurant. These are small changes, but I believe they will make a big difference in our family's health and well-being.

Why else might children be overweight? Some suggest that childhood obesity rates are skyrocketing with the rise in consumption of highly processed foods and the growing popularity of fast-food restaurants. We've all noticed that there are many more McDonald's, Burger Kings, Kentucky Fried Chickens, Domino's, and other fast-food outlets around. In his book *Fast Food Nation*, Eric Schlosser notes that McDonald's opens 2,000 new restaurants a year worldwide, or about 40 per week.

It's also incredible how many people are buying fast food. Consumers spent an estimated $110 billion on fast food in 2000. That's almost four times what the U.S. government spent on medical research in the same year.

Even food eaten at home has changed substantially. With the rise in the number of households where both parents work outside the home, parents have less time to buy and prepare food. The average time for meal preparation and consumption has dropped precipitously over the past decade, and this clearly has led to a difference in what kids eat.

In a nationally representative survey conducted in 1996–1998, researchers reported that more than 60 percent of kids ate five servings of fruits and vegetables a day. Unfortunately, these results were based on a very broad definition of vegetables that included potatoes, particularly french fries. When french fries were removed from the survey results, the percentage of children who consumed five servings of fruits and vegetables a day dropped to 30 percent. Potatoes fried in oil, usually trans fat oil, should not be considered a vegetable. More recently, in a survey conducted in 2001, researchers found that only 20 percent of U.S. children averaged five servings of fruits and vegetables a day.

When you take increased television watching, decreased physical activity, greater consumption of overprocessed foods and foods from fast-food restaurants, and lower consumption of fruits and vegetables among our children, the combined effect is a "perfect storm" of circumstances that are driving the childhood obesity epidemic.

LONG-TERM HEALTH CONSEQUENCES OF OVERWEIGHT

Unlike the cold or runny nose a child may catch at preschool, the pernicious onset of obesity can cause a lifetime of adverse health conditions (see "Health Consequences of Childhood Obesity").

How do we know that childhood obesity can cause a lifetime of health problems? Thanks to epidemiologists who focus on pediatric populations, we have the data to show this. A wonderful example is the Bogalusa Heart

Figure 2.2
Obesity Trend, Childhood to Adulthood

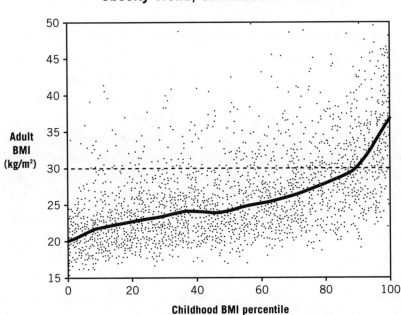

Childhood BMI percentile

Reprinted from Freedman, D.S. et al. (2001). Relationship of
childhood obesity to coronary heart disease risk factors in adulthood:
The Bogalusa Heart Study. *Pediatrics* 108 (3) : 712–718.

Study, one of the longest-running large-scale investigations of obesity
among children. Researchers followed a group of 16,000 children from
birth to almost 40 years of age and documented the tracking of childhood
obesity to adult obesity and adult chronic diseases. Among one sample of
children examined first between the ages of 2 and 17 and then again 17
years later, 77 percent of the children who were overweight (more than 95
percent for BMI) at baseline—that is, when the study began—were still
obese at follow-up. In contrast, only 7 percent of the normal-weight kids
were obese as adults 17 years later.

In figure 2.2, each dot represents a child's baseline BMI percentile for
their age plotted against their attained adult BMI. This shows that not all
overweight children were destined to become obese adults, nor were all

obese adults once overweight kids. However, the bold line represents the average trend of obesity in childhood to obesity later in life.

This trend is quite troubling, and suggests that rates of obesity among adults could skyrocket in future decades. If the percentage of obese children has tripled in just 2 decades in the United States, then this data from Bogalusa suggests that there may be a parallel tripling of rates of obesity among adults before 2020. Many studies document the association between childhood obesity and high levels of cholesterol, blood pressure, and blood sugar. The relatively tight tracking of childhood obesity to adult obesity means that these problems, too, will track into adulthood.

Now I want to take a closer look at what I consider the most worrisome medical consequences of the childhood obesity epidemic: diabetes and heart disease. Diabetes, a chronic and eventually crippling disease, is now diagnosed at alarming rates in younger and younger children. Heart disease is now, and has been for decades, the number-one killer of men and women.

The Increased Risk of Diabetes

As the seventh leading cause of death in the United States, diabetes is one of the leading causes of other chronic diseases, such as heart disease, stroke, and blindness. Approximately 10 percent of cases of diabetes are caused by an immunologic response in which the body destroys cells in the pancreas that make insulin, which is essential for the body to properly utilize energy. This is typically called type 1 diabetes and is not necessarily associated with obesity.

The remaining 90 percent of the estimated 16 million people in the United States with diabetes have what's called type 2 diabetes. Type 2 diabetes is related almost entirely to obesity or obesity-related factors. This condition is a more slowly progressive disease in which the body becomes resistant to insulin's biological signal.

Historically, type 1 diabetes was called juvenile diabetes because it was, and still is, diagnosed mostly among children and young adults. Alternatively, type 2 diabetes was classified as adult-onset diabetes. However, with the rise in obesity among children, the clinical signs and complications that typically were previously identified only in overweight 40- to 80-year-olds are being diagnosed now in children as young as 10 to 15 years of age.

It is estimated that 30 to 50 percent of cases of newly diagnosed diabetes among children are type 2. The life-altering complications and disabilities associated with type 2 diabetes are now affecting children and young adults. In addition, complications that can result from diabetes—such as eye problems, kidney disease, and high blood pressure—are also being diagnosed at unprecedented rates among children.

Heavy Hearts Lead to Heart Disease

Heart disease is a complicated condition with multiple causes, but it is thought to have its origins in atherosclerosis, the buildup of lipids and hardened plaques in the coronary arties. In the Bogalusa Heart Study, researchers were startled to find evidence of fatty streaks in the coronary arteries of obese children as young as 4 or 5 years of age. These fatty streaks are the early precursors to atherosclerosis and suggest that overweight children who stay overweight will have early-onset coronary disease.

While there are still no 50- and 60-year studies to tell us that obese children are more likely to experience higher rates of heart attacks later in life, the available evidence suggests that obese children have all of the other health complications in adolescence and young adulthood that will lead to heart disease. So it's not a stretch to imagine that rates of heart disease will soon increase rapidly among younger adults as the obese children of the 1970s and 1980s grow into their thirties, forties, and fifties.

YOUR CHILD'S PSYCHOLOGICAL HEALTH

Only recently has solid research emerged on the role of obesity in depression and overall quality of life. Twenty years ago, the biggest weight-related concerns among school nurses and psychologists were binge eating and purging among teenage girls. For many children, these complicated and serious eating disorders—bulimia and anorexia nervosa—could be identified and addressed, although treatment and health consequences can last for decades and, in the case of anorexia, put children and young adults at a much higher risk of early death.

However dangerous and critical these eating disorders are, it's interesting to note that estimates of their prevalence are substantially lower than the prevalence estimates of childhood obesity. That is not to say the severity of eating disorders should be ignored or stressed any less, but the impact of obesity on the mental state of our children should also not go unnoticed. As detailed in the book's remaining chapters, obesity and overweight can play havoc with your child's emotional health, causing academic, social, physical, and other problems.

As was mentioned in chapter 1, in an effort to figure out how obesity can affect a child's quality of life, researchers recently studied the emotional, social, and school functioning of 5- to 18-year-olds in California; 106 of the children were obese, 400 were healthy and of normal weight, and 106 had cancer. Each child and parent completed a 23-item questionnaire, which was used to calculate scores for psychosocial functioning.

The findings emphasize the urgency of this public health epidemic for children both psychologically and physically. The obese children and the parents of obese children were four to five times more likely to have impaired health-related quality-of-life scores than the healthy children. Even more surprising: The quality of life for the obese children was as bad as or even worse than what the children with cancer reported. Think about that— the onset of childhood obesity was as emotionally life-altering as contracting a terminal illness.

WHAT CAN WE DO?

So, what can we do? After reading this chapter, you may feel this is a daunting task to tackle. But there are many steps that parents, teachers, and public health officials can take. For example, new programs that integrate public health education with the daily school curriculum are being devel-

(continued on page 32)

GUIDELINES FOR CARDIOVASCULAR HEALTH PROMOTION IN ALL CHILDREN AND ADOLESCENTS

Health Promotion Goals	Recommendations
DIET	
• An overall healthy eating pattern	• Assess diet at every visit.
• Appropriate body weight	• Match energy intake with energy needs for normal growth and development.
• Desirable lipid profile	• Make appropriate changes to maintain a healthy weight and achieve weight loss when indicated.
• Desirable blood pressure	• Advocate consumption of a variety of fruits, vegetables, whole grains, dairy products, fish, legumes, poultry, and lean meat.
	• Fat intake is unrestricted prior to 2 years of age. After age 2, limit foods high in saturated fats (<10 percent of calories per day), cholesterol (<300 mg per day), and trans fatty acids.
	• Limit salt intake to <6 g per day.
	• Limit intake of sugar.
SMOKING	
• No new initiation of cigarette smoking	• Question tobacco use by parents at every visit.

Health Promotion Goals	Recommendations
SMOKING (*cont.*)	
• No exposure to environmental tobacco smoke	• Question tobacco use by children at every visit starting at age 10.
• Complete cessation for those who smoke	• Provide clear, strong, informed, and personalized counseling against initiation of smoking.
	• Advise avoidance of secondhand smoke at home, with friends, at school, and at work.
PHYSICAL ACTIVITY	
• Be physically active every day	• Assess physical activity at every visit.
• Reduce sedentary time (for example, television watching, computer, video games, or time on the phone)	• Advise young people to participate in at least 60 minutes of moderate to vigorous physical activity every day.
	• Physical activity should be fun for children and adolescents.
	• For adolescents, resistance training (10 to 15 repetitions at moderate intensity) can be combined with aerobic activity in an overall activity program.
	• Sedentary time should be limited. For example, limit television time to at most 2 hours per day.

Reprinted from Kavey, R.W. et al. (2003). AHA Scientific Statement: American Heart Association guidelines for primary prevention of atherosclerotic cardiovascular disease beginning in childhood. *Circulation* 107 (11): 1562.

oped and tested. One such educational tool—the Eat Well and Keep Moving program at the Harvard School of Public Health—is an interdisciplinary elementary school program designed to promote healthful eating and physical activity in schools, homes, and communities. This program has many unique aspects and is designed to have little cost to school systems and to require no extra staff. After a test of the program, elementary school children in the Baltimore school system ate less saturated fat, watched less TV, ate more fruits and vegetables, and knew more about nutrition and public health. Plus, the community support that programs like this provide only enhances what you're encouraging at home, so hopefully such programs will have a strong impact on slowing the rapid increase in childhood obesity. (See the appendix for more details on this worthwhile program.)

Thankfully, there has also been a recent push to remove junk food for sale at schools. In 2002, Los Angeles County voted for a 1- to 2-year phaseout of the sale of soft drinks to its 750,000 enrolled students. Some machines will be restocked with bottled water to defray lost revenue, and others will be eliminated.

Similar efforts are under way in New York City as well. If we consider the impact of a single 12-ounce can of cola on weight gain, as described earlier in this chapter, these measures may have an important ripple effect on weight gain among children in this large metropolitan area. Even if the cola itself does not lead to weight gain—because children either exercise more or do not eat calories from other sources—it provides only "empty calories," calories without nutrients. Research now tells us that many children, even those who are not overweight, get too much of their caloric needs from soda and are undernourished with regard to essential vitamins and minerals.

Regardless, moving soda and candy machines or other access to empty calories off school campuses seems like such an obvious public health statement that every school board or legislature should be pushing for these changes. Sure, schools may need extra revenue, but let's be creative and sell water or healthier choices, and *not* use the schools as an opportunity to make money from a vulnerable population at the expense of their lifetime health.

There has also been a national push to educate health professionals about the health burden of childhood obesity and to provide guidance for them. For example, the American Heart Association recently released guidelines to help health professionals identify children at risk (see "Guidelines for Cardiovascular Health Promotion in All Children and Adolescents" on page 30). Even though these guidelines are written for physicians, I suggest you bring this table to your child's next doctor's visit so you can set up a program together.

It is clear that childhood obesity is at epidemic levels and appears to be growing at alarming rates. Unless the problem is addressed and efforts are made on many fronts, the next generation is destined to see a precipitous rise in the chronic disease burden from diabetes, heart disease, cancer, and numerous other serious health consequences. While we tackle the physical problems on a national, statewide, and local level, it's up to parents like you and me to not forget about the mental state of children today. I am convinced that with the proper emotional support and participation from family members, children can be protected from not only the debilitating physical toll of being overweight, but its mental toll as well. Despite the frightening evidence presented in this chapter (or maybe because of it), you will be encouraged by the following chapters, where you will find exactly what you can do to help your children protect their emotional lives while you work to reverse the factors that are causing them to be overweight.

CHAPTER 3

FEELING LIKE A BLOB AND AN OUTCAST:
Emotional and Social Sorrows

In a society that prioritizes physical attractiveness and beauty, and equates that beauty with being excruciatingly thin, overweight children are at a great disadvantage and are vulnerable to difficult self-esteem issues and incredible peer pressure. Just as clearly as Eric's research points to physical challenges, my research findings demonstrate astounding emotional and social challenges for overweight children. Talking to current middle schoolers and interviewing adults who were fat as children revealed how terrible overweight children feel about themselves. And that is compounded by the ridicule and abuse overweight children get from their peers.

The enormity of the problem for overweight kids may be invisible to adults and children who are not heavy, but it can be overwhelming to overweight children and their parents.

PART I—THE FINDINGS

For every single social-emotional variable related to children's worries and confidence, overweight children fared worse than those of average weight. My survey found:

- Overweight children are much less likely than average-weight children to describe themselves as happy or cool, funny or confident.
- Overweight children are much more likely than average-weight children to describe themselves as lonely or sad, fearful or different.
- Overweight children are five times more likely than average-weight children to describe their self-confidence as poor.
- The more girls perceive they weigh, the less likely they are to describe themselves as beautiful or popular.
- Average-weight boys are 50 percent more likely than *very* overweight boys to describe themselves as athletic.
- Overweight children reported they had much greater worries than average-weight children. Three times the percentage of very overweight children were worried about their future compared to average-weight children. With few exceptions, no matter what topic we asked them about, overweight kids worried more about it than their average-weight peers.

SELF-ESTEEM

Children are not healthfully heavy, nor are they typically happily heavy. The myth of joviality associated with fat children is exactly that—a myth. In my survey, overweight children much less frequently described themselves as funny, happy, cool, or confident (see figure 3.1 on page 36) and more frequently described themselves as different, troublemaker, lonely, sad, fearful, and wimpy than average-weight children (see figure 3.2 on page 37). Self-esteem has many components beyond these self-descriptions, but the fact that overweight children so vividly describe themselves in such a negative light shows that their self-esteem is seriously at risk.

The negative self-assessment differs somewhat by gender. For boys, it was about being athletic. Overweight boys described themselves as athletic less frequently than did average-weight boys (53 percent, compared with 70 percent). Girls seemed more concerned with beauty and popularity; over-

Figure 3.1
Positive Self-Description, by Weight Category

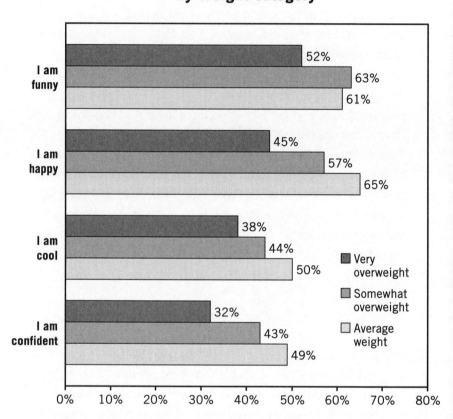

weight girls described themselves as beautiful (33 percent) or popular (26 percent) less frequently than did average-weight girls (46 percent and 33 percent, respectively). Indeed, the relationship between weight and perceived attractiveness couldn't have been clearer: The thinner the girls perceived themselves to be, the more frequently they described themselves as beautiful and popular.

Figure 3.3 on page 38 shows how middle-grade children's perceptions

Figure 3.2
Negative Self-Description, by Weight Category

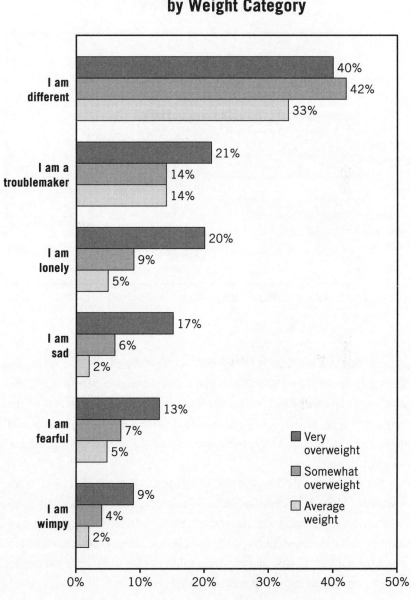

Figure 3.3
Self-Confidence Level,
by Weight Category

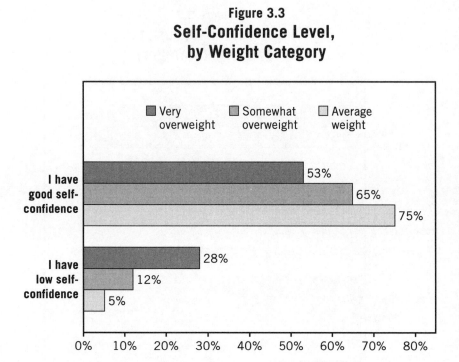

of their weight were directly related to how they rated their self-confidence. The more overweight the children perceived themselves, the more likely they were to describe their self-confidence as low. Some 28 percent of the very overweight kids and 12 percent of the somewhat overweight kids said they had low self-confidence, compared with only 5 percent of the average-weight children.

My survey results echo the findings of research conducted by Richard S. Strauss, M.D., a specialist in pediatric gastroenterology at the University of Medicine and Dentistry in New Jersey. He found that obese children with lowered self-esteem were more likely to be sad, lonely, and nervous. It's also true that sad, lonely, and nervous children were more likely to turn to food for emotional support for their loneliness.

Did you know that there are physiological reasons for craving carbohydrates when stressed? Stress causes serotonin levels in the blood to decrease, which then causes craving for carbohydrates. Foods rich in carbohydrates, those sweets that children turn to for comfort, raise serotonin levels and cause sad children to feel better, at least temporarily. Yet these carbs increase heavy children's weight problems and perpetuate their emotional crises. They gain more weight and have lower self-esteem, thus continuing a familiar cycle of sadness.

PEER REJECTION

While parents often minimize their children's weight problems by referring to them as "on the heavy side" or "a little chubby," the negative self-descriptions of overweight children reflect the negative terms their peers frequently used to describe them. The men and women I interviewed remembered with sad emotions a long list of names with which they were taunted, including Fatty Patti, Miss Piggy, Flabby Gabi, Tub of Lard, Mad Cow Disease, Fat Ass, Lard Butt, El Blimpo, and of course Fatso, Fatty, and Chubs. Even when they weren't called names, they often felt they didn't fit in or weren't accepted by others. Middle schoolers in my focus groups confirmed that negative nicknames continue today. For overweight boys, the description of "gay" or "fag" is often added to the taunts, which is hurtful to both the overweight children and to boys who may indeed believe they are homosexual.

The adults I interviewed vividly remembered their middle and high school years with sorrow. Nina first became sensitive to her overweight when kids started dating, in sixth grade. Nina wasn't teased, but she was rejected from the dating circle, never having had a single date.

Lorie recalled having a crush on her first boyfriend in fifth grade, only to be humiliated when he described her as "waddling to school."

Gail remembered that kids always assured her that she had a "pretty face," which for her implied the lack of a pretty body. Gail was gregarious, outgoing, and "one of the boys," but had no boyfriends or dates. She found that not having a boyfriend, when all her girlfriends did, was excruciating, particularly since she was always fixing other people up on dates and listening to her pals' love life problems. To mask her loneliness, she played the role of "party host," and kids thronged to her parties, permitting her to feel close to peers. Yet these parties had another, darker purpose; she could serve plenty of junk food—which she wouldn't dare eat in front of her friends, but could gorge on after the party ended.

Yet a large number of the adults I interviewed who had successfully taken control of their weight were able to accomplish this during middle and high schools, despite the daunting peer pressure (see "Miss Piggy Changes Her Image").

And today many obstacles remain. The adolescent boys in my focus groups laughed hilariously and displayed not an ounce of kindness as they described "fat" girls. One can only cringe at the emotional pain the girls they described must be feeling if these boys' comments are reflective of how they treat the overweight girls in their class.

"Fat girls try to wear tight shirts and the fat rolls hang out. They look nasty. They want to be like the good-looking girls, and they can't look good. They say, 'We know you want us, but don't touch,' and who wants to touch them?"

"So if there is a dance, it's always the ugly fat girls who want to talk to us. It's never the pretty, thin girls. The pretty girls don't have to work for what they want, and we have to go ask them to dance."

The focus group wasn't quite as cruel when they described overweight boys, but the raucous laughter with which they sang out their descriptions was not empathic laughter for their overweight friends, but laughter at their expense.

"Fat kids get teased most in gym (laughter). Even the coaches and gym teachers make fun of them. They're so clumsy, you'd better stay away from them. If they fall in gym, you'll get smooshed just like a pancake (more laughter)."

Rob, an overweight seventh-grader, shared the following story. (He undoubtedly felt miserable, but perhaps not as degraded as poor Maria, a sixth-grader.)

MISS PIGGY CHANGES HER IMAGE

The boys first called Phyllis Miss Piggy, but the girls, wanting to be included by the boys, soon joined in the taunting. The laughter hurt, and despite her brave front at school, Phyllis would cry and lash out at her family when she got home. At 5 feet 5 inches tall and almost 200 pounds, she'd sneak ice cream from the freezer and surreptitiously eat whatever junk food she could find. She had a few supportive friends, who would say "Don't worry about your weight. We like you anyway." Her parents said she'd work it out, and with their support she finally said to herself, "I'm really fat; I need to do something about this."

Phyllis joined a Weight Watchers group in seventh grade and found she could relate to the other adolescents in the group. By exercising and changing her eating habits, she lost 70 pounds during seventh and eighth grades.

By high school she was very thin and dealt with a few symptoms of eating disorders. However, she soon realized she was on the wrong path and stopped herself before getting out of control. Strangely enough, when she became thin in high school, there was more peer pressure. The boys were nice to her, but some girls taunted her for being too thin. She finally realized they were jealous, and it didn't bother her because she felt healthy and good about herself.

"So Mad I Could Explode"

I'm not much interested in girlfriends, but the guys make fun of me anyway. They laugh at me and tell me that Maria is in love with me. Maria is the fattest kid in the school, and she's pretty mean, too. She doesn't like me, and I don't like her. Actually, hardly anyone likes Maria, but the guys sing songs about how she loves me, how I love her, and how they saw me kiss her. They try to get me mad, and sometimes I feel so mad I could explode. Even when I walk away, they follow me and sing about Maria.

Rob, seventh grade

The adolescent girls in my focus groups were more sensitive with their descriptions of overweight peers, but clearly acknowledged that overweight boys had problems, as illustrated by the story of the description of Thomas by seventh-grader Angelee. Angelee showed some sensitivity to Thomas's feelings, but the girls could also be insensitive, as with Trina, a sixth-grader.

"I Know Thomas Will Never Forget . . ."

The coach had the boys playing basketball—skins and shirts. Thomas, my good friend, was on the skins team. He has big breasts, like a girl, and when he started running with the ball, his breasts bounced up and down. His face turned red, and he put his arms over his chest to cover himself. All the kids were talking about Thomas's breasts. Then the coach noticed and told him to put his shirt on, but I know Thomas will never forget what happened that day.

Angelee, seventh grade

"Kids Think I'm Dirty"

When kids have to pick partners in school or gym, no one picks me. The teacher always has to assign me a partner. The kids won't sit with me on the bus; they say I have lice. I don't have lice and I'm always clean about myself, but somehow kids always think I'm dirty just because I'm overweight.

Trina, sixth grade

BEING DIFFERENT AND OVERWEIGHT: DOUBLE JEOPARDY

When the interviewed adults had other differences considered negative by peers in addition to their overweight, the "other differences" seemed to encourage peers to taunt them even more. Being too tall or too brainy, wearing glasses, and having a learning disability or a lisp were some of those "different" characteristics that fueled more energy and anger among taunters.

Sally, an adult interviewee, suffered a triple whammy in school. She was the tallest in her class, was the only one who wore glasses, and weighed about 170 pounds by seventh grade. Her classmates called her Goggle Gobbler—"goggle" for her glasses, "gobble" to describe how she supposedly ate. And since she dressed in jeans and men's shirts to hide her fat, she also acquired the additional nickname Weirdo for her cover-up clothing. Not surprisingly, she felt totally unconnected to her peers.

Giftedness in combination with overweight increases the taunting for differences. In many middle schools, the term "brain" conjures up as much negativity by kids as the term "fat." For some reason, being intelligent seems to lose value during early adolescence. Matt, the eighth-grader from chapter 1, was tall, overweight, and brainy—another triple hex. Matt's mother shared his sad story with me.

Gifted and Lonely

Matt first grew "off the charts" when he was 3 years old, and he has been off them ever since. In fourth and fifth grades, kids smaller than Matt would gang up on him on the playground and try to see how many it would take before they could knock him down or get him to react. If he did react, by swinging his arm to get the kids off his neck or back, they would cry and claim Matt had hurt them. At first it was hard for the playground supervisors to understand that this big kid had *not* been the aggressor.

When Matt was in sixth grade, he met a new group of kids in his new school. He was the biggest kid in the school at 5 feet 10 inches tall and 220 pounds. In fact, he was bigger than the principals and teachers, too. Kids would walk down the hall between classes when teachers were not watching, poke Matt in the stomach, and say, "Hey, Doughboy. Hey, Pillsbury Doughboy." The kids sensed that he would not be egged into a fight with them, so the insults escalated. Each new slur was intended to see how much he could take.

One time on the playground, in order to defend a smaller friend who was getting punched, Matt shoved a boy and got into a fight. A supervisor took Matt directly to the school office, where he was severely reprimanded for fighting with a smaller student, while the smaller student, who had attacked Matt's friend, was treated sympathetically.

Matt is an easygoing person, likes attention, and wants to be friends with everyone. He is also very verbal and has a huge vocabulary. Because of his size and his unusual vocabulary, Matt was an easy target. He was often the target of jokes because he didn't have a vocabulary that included swear words or slurs. Instead, he would try Shakespearean humor, which his peers didn't understand.

Wanting to be liked, he hung out with a group of guys who would bait him with questions. Once he was asked, "Which do you like better? *Playgirl* or *Playboy*?" Thinking the right answer would involve girls, he said, "I don't know, *Playgirl*," and then the guys laughed and called him "gay."

I talked to Matt as well. In eighth grade now, he is 6 feet tall and weighs 260 pounds. His pessimism and pain were palpable in our interview. He appears mature for his age, looks like a 16-year-old, and interacts comfortably with adults, but when he's surrounded by five or six small 13-year-olds who take turns taunting him, he responds like any 13-year-old might and loses control by hitting out at them. They're quick to complain to the principal, and their stories of bullying are more believable because of their small size. It's hard for the administrators to imagine a 6-foot-tall, manlike child being bullied by these small children. The boys in wrestling took a special pride in taunting Matt. Read Matt's account of what happened.

I guess it's like a passage of honor for some of the wrestlers to tackle me. They'll come at me in herds, and one of them will ask me if I want to wrestle. I usually refuse. I'll turn around to walk away, and they'll hit me. Then I'll turn around and say, "Fine. I'll take you down." Then they'll get in this weird wrestling stance and they'll jump at me and tackle my legs. I'll end up falling on the ground, and they'll try to grab my neck. One time Joseph had a choke hold on me. I stood up, picked him up, and flipped him backward and landed on him. I don't want to hurt people, but if they tackle me and they're hurting me, I will hurt them back. So I pushed Joseph away, and all the other wrestlers got mad at me and circled around me. Joseph couldn't wrestle me anymore, so then Scott came in and started wrestling me. Next Alex came in. The group would circulate through people so they always had a person that wasn't so tired to try to wear me down. I had to keep on going until finally I kneed Alex in the stomach so he'd get off of me. He was lying there, and then I got into trouble.

Matt, eighth grade

WORRIES FOR OVERWEIGHT CHILDREN

It's no wonder that overweight children worry more. Much of their peer world rejects them. Overweight girls worry more than overweight boys; this perhaps is a reflection of the greater cruelty toward overweight girls than boys or is because somewhat overweight boys seem to sometimes find an acceptable place in sports. Overweight boys still worry more than average-weight boys do, probably because they are also victimized more by others.

"Social/Emotional Worries (Girls)" and "Social/Emotional Worries (Boys)" on pages 46 and 47 demonstrate that overweight children worry much more than average-weight children. The survey asked children to indicate only those things that they worried about *frequently*. The charts list the worries in order of what very overweight children worried about most.

Popularity and Attractiveness

Worries about popularity with the opposite sex were much more frequent for girls than for boys. While almost twice the percentage of overweight girls as average-weight girls worried about popularity with boys, the boys' worries about popularity with girls didn't vary much by weight group. That may be related to boys' later maturation and lesser interest in girls at that age.

Many very overweight and somewhat overweight girls also worried about not being pretty enough, compared with average-weight girls. For boys, the greatest worry about personal attractiveness was indicated only by those in the very overweight group. A somewhat overweight boy may be considered big and strong (an advantage for males) and not be considered as unattractive as a very overweight boy.

SOCIAL/EMOTIONAL WORRIES (GIRLS), BY WEIGHT CATEGORY

	Very overweight %	Overweight %	Average weight %
I'm too fat	82	74	24
I'm not pretty enough	48	46	26
I feel pressure to have nice clothes	46	44	29
Popularity with boys	41	32	22
Popularity with girls	40	46	30
I don't have enough self-confidence	39	30	16
People who bully me	33	15	11
Loneliness	30	23	14
I'm not social enough	28	21	16
My friends don't understand me	20	18	12
I'm too bossy	20	18	14
I feel pressure to think about sex	19	19	11
I'm too tall	15	12	8

Many of the adult women interviewed described themselves as having felt ugly as young girls. Even into adulthood, although they were of normal weight or only slightly overweight, their fear of being overweight still plagued them. Their internalized image from childhood was of an overweight person, and even their current healthy lifestyles could not eradicate that self-perception.

Clothing

Worries about clothing were often what alerted the adult interviewees in childhood to their being different from other children. Not surprisingly, the

SOCIAL/EMOTIONAL WORRIES (BOYS), BY WEIGHT CATEGORY

	Very overweight %	Overweight %	Average weight %
I'm too fat	68	45	6
Popularity with girls	32	31	27
Popularity with boys	25	20	20
I'm not handsome enough	24	8	3
I'm not social enough	20	17	12
I feel pressure to think about sex	20	14	11
People who bully me	19	13	13
Loneliness	15	13	9
I don't have enough self-confidence	15	14	9
I feel pressure to drink alcohol	15	11	9
My friends don't understand me	12	10	7
I'm too tall	10	4	3

worries about pressure to have nice clothes were more frequently a girl's concern. Shopping for clothes was a special chore. It was difficult finding clothes in the "big kids," "chubby," or "husky" department, where there wasn't much variety or style. Terri remembered her clothing dilemma.

Terri Felt like a Million Bucks

In seventh grade I needed a dress for a special party. I was one big roly-poly. My father suggested I try "Omar the tent maker." I became accustomed to his jokes. My mom persevered, though, taking me to a zillion stores, but there was nothing to be found. I was in tears by the end of the day, but not my mother. She was furious at the designers who weren't making clothes for girls who were "a little chunky." She said, "Screw the designers. I'll make you a beautiful dress." And she did. She sewed me a black velvet A-line jumper and worked on it every day in order to get it done on time. She even let me help with the sewing, and I loved that. Then she bought me a woman's blouse and changed all the buttons to sparkling rhinestones. When I went to the party, I felt like a million bucks.

Hot pants were also in style then. As I was 5 feet 3 inches tall and at least 150 pounds, they were a little tight-fitting for me, but my mom found outfits of stretch polyester with long tunic tops. She had gone through this same problem when she was my age, and she wasn't going to let my weight get me down.

Terri, adult interviewee

While Terri's mother identified with Terri's problem and was supportive, Gail's mom didn't even take her shopping. Perhaps shopping for Gail and her four overweight sisters was too burdensome. Gail's mom would purchase clothes without Gail's input, and unfortunately she didn't have a very good sense of what styles looked best for overweight girls. Instead of a more flattering A-line dress, Gail was given pleated plaid skirts and gathered dresses, which accentuated her overweight. The clothes were stylish, but not flattering to Gail, and certainly not her choice. They only made things worse, and she felt embarrassed wearing them.

While many women interviewed became aware of their weight problems because of the difficulty of finding clothes, only one man commented on the clothing dilemma. Harry recalled having to go to the "husky shop" for pants because he couldn't fit into the hand-me-down pants of his thin brother. That bothered him, but was nothing compared with the way the girls suffered with clothing.

The middle schoolers in my focus groups insisted that clothes are more important today than they were for their parents. Fifth- through eighth-graders claimed that the right brand names and styles were imperative for acceptance by popular kids. The middle schoolers in urban schools wore more hip-hop clothes, which in their bagginess might be better for overweight children, but the kids still had to look cool in the right look to fit in.

Bullying and Loneliness

Girls more frequently indicated worries about loneliness, being bullied, and lack of self-confidence than the boys, and the stories told earlier in this chapter corroborate that gender difference. (In general, girls of all weight categories worried more than boys.) Nevertheless, most of these worries varied by weight for boys as well, with overweight boys being more likely than average-weight boys to state their concerns. (Matt's story of being bullied showed how lonely and isolating it must have felt to be attacked by a group of kids.)

Sex and Being Too Fat

The frequency with which overweight girls and boys felt pressure to think about sex could be directly related to their perceived earlier development; this is discussed in chapter 6. The greatest worry for both girls and boys was their concern about being too fat. That, too, was worse for girls than boys. Yet the overweight children didn't worry about how unhealthy it is to be overweight; rather, they worried about the peer rejection their weight caused. It would have been good if that worry led to healthy eating and exercise, but as you can see from the stories I encountered, worrying alone is rarely helpful.

Their Future

In my survey, I asked children how optimistic or anxious they felt about their future. My research found overweight children indicated less optimism and more anxiety about their future (see figure 3.4 on page 50), with three times the number of very overweight children more concerned than average-weight children.

It's not a particular surprise that overweight children are more pessimistic and worried about their future. The negative effects of peer and

Figure 3.4
Optimism and Anxiety about the Future, by Weight Category

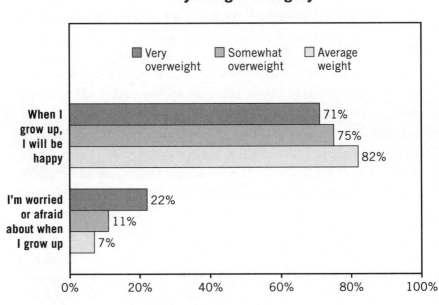

adult rejection cause serious harm. Dislike and disapproval of fat children continues to be a sadly acceptable prejudice. The world has not treated them fairly or well, and that ill treatment can dampen their future aspirations.

Figure 3.5 on page 52 shows the dramatic differences in priorities for the future between very overweight children and average-weight children. Very overweight children were less likely to be concerned about challenge and creativity in their careers, perhaps because fewer believed they could respond to challenge successfully. They also cared less about making the world a better place. Instead they were more focused on fame and fortune, which reflects the "magical thinking" often typical of overweight children. Children who believe they can't accomplish realistic goals may imagine that a fairy godmother will anoint them with fame and fortune.

The good news is that the children who described themselves as somewhat overweight indicated attitudes more similar to those of average-weight children, rather than the deeper pessimism of the very overweight children. Their continued optimism confirms that they may not have suffered as much peer or adult abuse as the very overweight children; they remain reasonably optimistic. While that offers no reassurances to parents of very overweight children, who are more at risk, it is reassuring to parents of children who are only somewhat overweight, provided that the parents can prevent their children's eventual obesity.

Family Life and the Prospects of Marriage

I found it very striking that average-weight children most frequently chose "a happy family life" (74 percent) as a priority, as compared to only 55 percent of the very overweight group. Very overweight children most frequently selected "earning a lot of money" (63 percent), perhaps because they were less likely to believe in the possibility of having a happy family life. And I also asked a marriage question, which isn't graphed here: more than twice the percentage of very overweight children (18 percent) indicated they didn't expect to marry compared to those who were somewhat overweight or average weight (8 percent). Could it be that even at early adolescence overweight children believed that they were so unattractive to the opposite sex that it would preclude a future marriage for them?

RESPONSES TO PEER TAUNTING

Adolescents and the adult interviewees as teenagers responded to peer taunting in a variety of ways, most of which were not effective. Sixth-grader Trina was lonely, isolated, and depressed and ate even more to keep the sadness away. Seventh-grader Rob felt furious and explosive and aimed his anger at his family. Amanda remembered pretending she didn't hear peer comments like "Oh, yeah, have another candy bar, Fat Ass." She'd say to herself, "Pretend you don't hear, pretend they didn't say that, don't let them see they hurt you, don't cry, don't let them see they got to you." She tried to ignore them, but the damage was already done. Amanda believed she was ugly, and internalized that image, and as an adult she still feels unattractive.

Figure 3.5
Priorities for the Future, by Weight Category

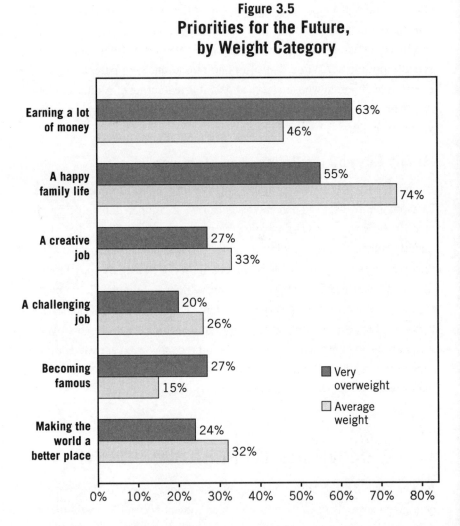

Susan recalled that she had a few female friends, but for the most part she didn't participate in playground activities. An only child, she returned home from school to be alone some more, eating and watching television to keep herself company. Her mother worked and didn't get home until late, and although her dad was home and cooked meals for the family, he instilled fear in Susan. Susan felt she could never do anything well enough to please him. She felt safest and most comfortable if she sat quietly, ate the food her dad cooked, and watched television. When both her parents were home, they joined her to eat meals in front of the TV set.

After years of being teased as Fatty Patti, Patti finally discovered kindness among her peers after a family tragedy. Patti's dad and brother were killed by a train while she was in grade school. When the community heard about the horrible accident, Patti's peers stopped teasing her. Of course, children shouldn't have to experience a tragedy in order for peers to be nice to them, but we need to make young people aware how they can hurt others with taunting.

Darlene remembers discovering the power within her to stop the peer abuse. In middle school, the boys teased her about her size. At first she felt like "a blob" and couldn't believe she was nice-looking or smart. She ate carbohydrates for comfort, didn't exercise, and had poor study habits, resulting in terrible grades. She recorded on her calendar each day she cried at school. After almost 2 years of grief, she looked at her calendar and thought, *This has got to stop.* She begged the girlfriends of the boys who were torturing her to make the boys stop. It worked—and the boys started being nice to her.

After this turn of events, one boy, who had been out sick for 5 weeks, came back to school and started to make fun of Darlene as had been his earlier habit. The ringleader told him to shut up. This was a turning point for Darlene as she realized she could do something to control the abuse. Later in high school she learned to respond quickly to mean comments by pointing out a weakness in a teaser. She recognized that bullies were usually covering up their own problems, and if she could embarrass bullies, they wouldn't bother her. She soon had little to worry about. Darlene's defense was effective and reduced the taunting, but she never forgot the earlier pain, nor did she ever feel genuinely accepted by those who had hurt her.

After many years of tears, Matt finally learned in the seventh grade that he could control some abuse from his peers. He joined the football team, where his size was an asset, as well as his smarts. Now the smaller guys looked to Matt for protection. At one practice the coach, trying to get Matt to be more aggressive, promised to reduce the team's laps if Matt could push the coach on a sled for 20 yards. He was able to do it, thereby endearing him to his teammates. His social status in school increased temporarily, and the high school coaches immediately started looking him over.

But Matt wasn't really interested in football, and his coach pushed him to be more aggressive, which was counter to his sensitive personality. Matt tried track and discovered that he could lose some weight with the regular running exercise. He liked that better and admitted that both sports resulted in a little more acceptance by peers, although neither sport made him an enthusiast. Furthermore, he hadn't completely rid himself of peers' teasing.

Of the adult interviewees, most remembered having overtly laughed with others about their weight, but feeling terribly hurt and lonely, crying when they came home, or complaining sadly to parents or friends. A few learned to take on their taunters with a sharp tongue, and their aggressive speech eventually kept the taunters at bay. The men we interviewed found sports as a way to become accepted by peers. Getting support from close friends was effective, especially if those allies were willing to stand up for them. For some, hosting parties or listening to the woes of other, more popular kids permitted friendships. Fifth-grader Stuart found support from a friend in a surprising way (see "Stuart Finds a Friend").

WHEN PEER PRESSURE HELPED

For adult interviewees Jeff, Ana, Terri, Phyllis, Nina, and Ralph, peer pressure had helped them to lose weight. Their wishes to fit in with peers or to be attractive to the opposite sex had motivated them to eat moderately and lead active lifestyles. Ultimately, losing weight and becoming involved in physical activities was most effective for warding off taunts.

Jeff was one adult interviewee who never considered himself overweight as a kid since he was well-coordinated and athletic. The kids called him Turk (the name of a powerful wrestler) and he was sociable, happy, and accepted. Positive peer pressure and his wish to stay socially successful helped him to take control of his weight problem.

STUART FINDS A FRIEND

Stuart was very tall, very large, and very lonely, and he was always the victim of plenty of taunting. When his teacher asked him to be the eyes for a blind boy in his class, Stuart took the responsibility seriously. The two boys became very close friends and soon went everywhere together. Strangely, once Stuart had a good friend, the taunting by his peers stopped completely.

Jeff Takes Control

I never considered myself fat until I was about 12 and my pediatrician announced that I was 70 pounds overweight. I argued with him and told him I couldn't possibly be that fat, although I reluctantly admitted I might be a little overweight. I continued to argue with him (I had a reputation for arguing), but I heard his message. The fact that a doctor was taking my weight seriously captured my attention. He prescribed an appetite suppressant and recommended a weight loss diet. Although the doctor helped get me started, what really motivated me to diet was that I had noticed girls. I knew the girls wouldn't like me if I was fat, so I started eating healthy foods. I lost 40 pounds after that. I've always struggled with weight problems, but I have learned to be moderate and careful of my diet. I also exercise regularly. Exercise was an important part of my life even as a child; I played a sport every season.

Jeff, adult interviewee

Nina's story is significant because her motivation to lose weight came from teen magazines. There are many negative aspects to teen magazines, including photographs of models who are excruciatingly thin and the predominating emphasis on fashion, makeup, sex, and girls' identities being tied to boyfriends. However, some parts of teen magazines can be helpful, and Nina learned to eat more healthfully and exercise from what she read.

Fashion Magazines Educated Nina

I was always in chubby clothes and was probably 30 pounds over-weight. I was very shy because of the weight issue, and I was never in the in crowd. I had only one good friend, but was never worried about having a problem when I was younger. I was a picky eater who ate no vegetables, but did eat plenty of junk food like Yankee Doodles, Yodels, and bacon sandwiches. No one exercised in my family, so of course I didn't either.

In ninth grade I started reading fashion magazines in the hopes of figuring out how to have a better social life, but I read about exercise and calories instead. I started writing down everything I ate and adding up the calories; I wouldn't let myself go over 1,200 calories a day. I did the situps and exercises recommended in the magazines and lost 25 pounds. My social life improved dramatically when I was thin. Once I could admit I was overweight, I was able to educate myself on how to do something about it, and it worked.

Nina, adult interviewee

Terri wanted a boyfriend, and that encouraged her to lose weight. She always knew she was fat when she was little, but it didn't bother her. Her whole "jolly" family was overweight, and they all liked to eat. Terri was incredibly social and had plenty of friends. Kids knew her and accepted her until she went to a large middle school, where new kids who didn't know her—and her being fat—kept peers away. Seventh and eighth grades were the most difficult, and she especially hated the way she looked in eighth grade. Terri remembered being upset because she would never let a boy put his arm around her waist because she was afraid of "what he would feel." She tried to get her family to join her in a family diet, but they refused. She wanted a boyfriend by ninth grade, so she dieted on her own and lost 20 pounds. By high school she wore a size nine, and she felt much better about herself. She had found it impossible to make new friends when she was fat before, but once kids got to know her, weight didn't make a difference, even when she gained some back. She was so happy in high school she never wanted to leave.

DENIAL OF OVERWEIGHT

All of the adult interviewees were in denial of their overweight until someone deliberately intervened or a defining experience changed their perspective and their behaviors related to weight. Jeff's story showed that he was in denial about his overweight when he argued with his pediatrician. A medical intervention started him on his lifelong road to personal weight control.

Despite teasing beginning in fourth and fifth grades, Nancy denied she was fat. She had a lisp and needed special speech therapy classes, another example of a double whammy of differences. Because of her absences from class, kids started calling her "retarded" and added "chunky," "chubby," and "fat" to the list of taunts. Everyone was always trying to put her on a diet. "Don't eat the Snickers bars" and "Stop eating that starchy stuff" were just a couple of the nagging reminders.

It wasn't until Nancy tried out for cheerleading in eighth grade that she accepted her problem. She was good at flips and had great coordination despite her overweight, but Miss Jones, the coach, told her she hadn't made the team because she was too fat. Nancy didn't get depressed; instead, she got angry. She said to herself, "Okay, this needs to come off. It's bad that people say I can't do stuff because I'm fat. That's never happening again." Finally, she accepted her problem and ate less and worked out more. Her new self-discipline made a difference in the rest of her life.

PART II—RESCUING TECHNIQUES

The emotional and social sadness overweight children experience causes the difficult issues I've described. Here I share techniques for helping them cope with peers. But these challenges are so formidable that we can't ex-

ALEX: DENIAL RUNS DEEP

I spoke with 11-year-old Alex, a sixth-grader who looked more like an overweight eighth- or ninth-grader. He described himself as happy, having plenty of friends, active in sports, enjoying challenge, and not at all worried about his weight. He said gym was his favorite class, and he enjoyed football, soccer, and basketball. He said he didn't worry about his weight because luckily he was "energetic and active." He told me he ate balanced meals with plenty of fruits and vegetables, although he confessed that his favorite food was hot dogs. He also said he loved pecans, which he claimed to carefully limit to 50 nuts a day. He described himself as an excellent student, earning A's and B's.

Descriptions of Alex by adults in his school suggested a very different young man. They explained that he had few friends and that kids barely tolerated him. He was never picked as a partner, but out of sensitivity to his feelings, teachers paired him with other children, instead of causing him the embarrassment of not being chosen. The teachers rotated his partners since his peers didn't want to be paired with him. Alex would hit or bump people "accidentally" and make up excuses for his annoying and intrusive behaviors. He also talked too much, ate food

pect children to cope with them alone. On the other hand, too much adult intervention is counterproductive because children will feel less confident if they become too dependent on adult assistance. So in your rescue operations on the emotional front, you will need to be sensitive to your child's feelings, his developmental stage, and his gradually increasing need for independence in order for him to build self-esteem.

This section guides you in helping your child to:

- Admit and accept that there's a weight problem
- Build self-esteem
- Delineate friendship and popularity and improve his or her social skills
- Develop independence without loneliness

off other children's plates, and angered easily, especially when things didn't go his way. He acted in ways that would attract negative or humorous "clowning" attention. Kids would laugh *at* him, not *with* him. Despite his statements to the contrary, he didn't play any school sports. Although Alex was highly intelligent, he often handed in his assignments late or not at all, and his grades reflected his inconsistent homework.

When his teachers shared their concerns with his single mother, who was also overweight, she denied that Alex had problems. She thought he was happy. She had so far refused to take him in for counseling or a medical evaluation related to his behavior or his overweight. I wondered if an event or a person would serve to change Alex's denial and encourage him to deal with his problems, or whether he would continue his growth toward obesity in continued denial. His perceptions of himself showed no resemblance to how others described him. It was as if he had no boundaries in most of his behaviors, and his lack of boundaries in eating was part of his personality problem. Neither he nor his mother recognized Alex's desperate need for boundaries, and both were ignoring his serious weight problem.

- Navigate the clothing issue
- Learn resilience and optimism
- Handle peer bullies
- Cope with depression

ADMITTING AND ACCEPTING THAT THERE'S A WEIGHT PROBLEM

Accepting that a weight problem is serious is the first step for a child to overcome her problem. Children in denial are not motivated to change. When a child is overweight, calling her "a little on the heavy side," "chunky," or "chubby" disguises the serious health problems she has and may continue to ignore. If she is overweight, be sure to tell her, but you don't need to remind her daily. Telling her not to eat fattening foods or to go easy on the sweets and starches while you continue to serve huge portions of pastas and desserts will not help her cope with her problems either. As a loving parent, envision yourself as a coach, and assure your child of your love and your concern for her health. Here are some tips for this difficult, private conversation.

- Confront your child with the fact that she is seriously overweight by saying, "I know you realize that you are seriously overweight, and you must feel bad about that."
- Form an alliance with your child on her path to a healthy lifestyle by telling her, "I want to help you to become healthy and to feel good about yourself."
- Use your knowledge of nutrition to teach your child about calories and balance in her diet, or learn together about proper nutrition (see the Web sites in the appendix).
- Teach your child about appropriate portion sizes.
- Serve healthy, balanced meals to the entire family.
- Assure your child of your confidence in her capability to set limits on her eating by saying, "I know you'll want to work on this problem at some time."
- Meet with a nutritionist for further guidance.
- Have your child evaluated by her doctor.
- Enroll your child in a children's weight control group.
- Teach your child about adopting an active lifestyle.
- Be a good role model for healthy eating and healthy activity.

Despite all you can do, you may find your child resisting your suggestions and denying her weight problem, in which case you will have to be patient. Your acceptance of your child's weight problem is the first step for her own acceptance. Acceptance of our children's weight problems, our love and allegiance for our children, our willingness to educate them as a coach, and most of all our patience while they learn to accept their weight problems are extremely important as we try to rescue children from their social and emotional sorrows and direct them to their inner strengths.

SELF-ESTEEM GROWS FROM RECOGNITION OF STRENGTHS AND TALENTS

The first part of this chapter showed that overweight children's lesser self-confidence stems from the negative stereotypes given to them by insensitive peers and adults. Direct praise to children and referential or indirect praise about them to other significant adults can act to counter the negative stereotypes and help raise children's expectations of themselves. The words used to describe children, directly or indirectly, become labels and often make for self-fulfilling prophecies. If children are labeled negatively, they often assume they are destined for those negative behaviors. On the other hand, if they hear positive descriptors, children try to live up to them. However, when positive descriptors are too extreme, children may feel it's impossible to achieve such high goals and may feel pressured. (See "Elizabeth the Beautiful" on page 62, which provides an example of this instance from my clinical work.)

My research dramatically showed that overweight children worried more than average-weight children about not being pretty, popular, social, or athletic enough. Even when people referred to their faces as beautiful, overweight children tended to take that as a backhanded compliment implying that their bodies were fat and ugly. You might think logically that praising children as beautiful, gorgeous, or stunning from early childhood on would prevent this and give them confidence in their attractiveness by the time they reach age 10 or 12. Actually, such overpraise typically backfires for all children, and this is especially so for overweight children, like Elizabeth. Children assume from your frequent use of extreme praise that attractiveness is the most important family priority and that their being overweight makes it impossible to live up to such high standards. If you emphasize beauty too much, your children may feel they can never please you

ELIZABETH THE BEAUTIFUL

Eighth-grader Elizabeth cried desperately to her mother about her wish to be prettier and thinner. Her mother reassured her that she was a very beautiful girl and that she had nothing to worry about. Instead of feeling comforted, Elizabeth lost her temper at her mother, exclaiming at the top of her voice, "I'm not beautiful! I'm not beautiful. I'll never be beautiful!"

When Elizabeth came in to see me and shared her anger, she told me she knew she wasn't beautiful and couldn't understand what her mother expected of her. I reassured her and explained that when she got dressed up and fixed her hair, she could look quite nice, and that was all we could expect. No matter how pretty girls are, sometimes they don't feel pretty enough. I encouraged her to take healthy care of her appearance, eat well, exercise regularly, and accept herself the way she was. I also explained to her that for parents, a child almost always seems beautiful because parents are evaluating the whole child, not just looks. That seemed to reassure Elizabeth, at least temporarily. I also suggested to her mother to be more moderate in her praise because it would seem more sincere to Elizabeth and not cause her to feel as much pressure.

or their peers. On the other hand, if every once in a while you mention that they look nice, cool, neat, or terrific, that's enough to build their confidence in their appearance without making it a high priority. Your children should be able to feel good about their appearance with occasional praise, but continual overpraise is likely to have the opposite effect.

Children also need praise for other qualities besides looks because praise conveys your values to your children. For instance, it's good to laugh at their jokes and tell them they have a good sense of humor, or to comment to your friend, while making sure your child overhears you, that your child has a terrific personality. Mention your children's strengths from time to time. Again, I want to reiterate that you should avoid praising children too extremely or too profusely; either it will not feel sincere to your children, as in Elizabeth's case, or they will think your expectations are too high. I don't wish to dampen your spontaneous enthusiasm about your children's successes, so if every once in a while you become genuinely very excited about their accomplishments, don't let me make you feel guilty. They will probably love it, and it's much more likely to do more good than harm as long as the praise isn't constant.

Children who receive no praise don't feel good about themselves. Furthermore, constant negative comments about being awkward, klutzy, ugly, fat, jealous, or mean cause children to feel helpless to conquer those negative stereotypes. Overweight children may already be bombarded by such nasty talk from others. Your positive descriptions have to be convincing enough so they can let others' negative comments deflect off them. When they hear negative comments from peers, their intuitive response, based on good self-esteem, can become "I'm okay, so what's your problem?"

Since so many of the self-esteem problems of overweight children are tied to appearance, it's good to establish a value system early that says "Pretty is as pretty does." By age 5 or 6, children can understand that their actions are more impressive than whether they are pretty or not. Learning to equate beauty with being kind, helpful, smart, and strong rather than with being thin, wearing makeup, or having brand-name clothes will go a long way toward helping your children thrive in adolescence and even into young adulthood. The foundation for that needs to be laid in childhood, before peer pressure communicates to your children in a voice louder than yours. Even if you've waited until middle school to communicate these values, your words will nevertheless be reassuring.

PEER PRESSURES, FRIENDSHIP, AND POPULARITY

Peer issues—including popularity, social skills, and worries about having the right clothes—all have to be addressed by the time kids enter middle school. This is often the most difficult time for overweight children because middle schoolers naturally want to fit in and be accepted.

Dispelling the Popularity Myth

If adults brag about their children's popularity or admire popular children in other families, children pick up the idea that being popular is an important value. If teachers discuss students' popularity with parents, parents may assume that being popular is a priority, and then communicate that value to their children.

By middle school, the "popular group" is a peer classification of the most accepted and powerful group in the school. Middle school children in my focus groups repeatedly talked about how much pressure they felt to be included and accepted by the popular kids. They described the popular group as so powerful that it controlled everyone, so if you weren't accepted or were taunted by popular kids, you were an outcast. They assured me that their parents could never have felt similar pressures in middle school. From the children's perspective, if popular kids taunt overweight kids, kids who are overweight will suffer rejection by others as well.

Your overweight child could have a terrible fear of being shunned by his powerful peers. It's important to be empathic to the pressures he's feeling and reassure him that popularity will not continue to hurt him as he matures. Your child will need confidence that he can be successful and happy, and have good friends, without being popular.

Improving Social Skills

Children do need friends, and they benefit from learning good social skills. If you teach your children social skills early, before peers are so negative toward children who are overweight, they will be more likely to develop the social confidence needed to navigate those difficult adolescent years. Even as a preschooler, your child can say, "Hi, I'm Cody. Do you want to play trucks?" or "Hello, I'm Allie. I brought my Barbie. Do you want me to share with you?" He or she can learn to say to a group of children who are already playing, "I'm new here, and my name is Hannah. Can I play with you?" These are phrases children are taught to use in child care or preschool, so it's good to introduce them to your children at home before they enter school. You can pretend you're Cody or Allie and practice role-playing with your children so they feel comfortable about joining others or inviting others to play. The concepts of sharing and taking turns have to be learned, but they go a long way toward helping children fit in.

Playdates for preschoolers and elementary-age children are important parts of their social learning. Not only do they help children feel comfortable with the roles of host and guest, they give parents the opportunity to observe their children at play. That observation provides the basis for teaching children what they need to know about getting along with others, as well as how to share and how to be assertive. You may need to teach a child how to say "You had a turn, and now it's my turn," as well as "I've had my turn, and now you can have yours" and even "You can have your turn first." If you don't watch your children play with other children, you won't know what they need to learn about getting along with others. Although many busy parents struggle with finding the time to arrange playdates, it's the best way to understand your child's social needs.

Social skills change as children mature, but even in middle and high schools you'll get a better picture of kids' interactions if you encourage them to invite friends to your home. Overweight children may struggle with finding friends that will come over, so you may suggest your child invite only one or two people so he doesn't face the fear of rejection. Help your tweens or teens plan some interesting activities with their friends—like cooking a meal together, working on crafts or a school project, roller skating, or even renting a special video—to give them some confidence for inviting friends. Parents who make their children's friends feel comfortable in their homes facilitate their children's getting return invitations. Keep in mind that it's hard on tweens when they're not invited to parties. They may have to issue three or four invitations before they receive one in return.

ENCOURAGING INDEPENDENCE

In addition to teaching children how to socialize, it's important to encourage them to entertain themselves. Children shouldn't depend on having friends or even siblings around all the time. It's good to teach them

DANIELLE LEARNS THAT POPULARITY ISN'T FRIENDSHIP

Here's a conversation Danielle, an overweight seventh-grader, had with her mother, and you could have with your child as well.

Danielle: (crying to her mom) Aaron and the guys were laughing at me again, and I tried to ignore them, but they made some comment about my rolls of fat showing. Ugh. How could they be so mean? I really hate them, but nobody else does. Everyone thinks they're so great. They're so popular that when they laugh at me, I feel like everyone's laughing at me. What makes them so popular?

Mom: I can tell you feel really bad, and I'm glad you tried to ignore them. I know it hurts, but hopefully they'll stop if you can ignore them long enough.

Danielle: But Mom, how come they're so lucky? They're so cool, and they wear the right clothes and they have the best parties. I wish they'd invite me, but that'll never happen. They laugh at other people, too, but nobody seems to mind. Mom, if I were popular, I'd never be that mean.

Mom: I know you wouldn't be, and popular kids aren't always mean. Sometimes they can be nice, and other times they keep their groups together only because

to feel comfortable playing alone so they can develop personal interests without feeling lonely. But this isn't a suggestion that your children fill this time with continuous and passive television viewing; that's a bad idea. Instead, try to encourage your child to participate in activities that are physically or intellectually challenging. Children's time alone can be spent shooting baskets, taking walks, running, riding a bike, creating crafts, reading a book, or writing a story. If children develop their own interests, they'll be less likely to feel depressed when they're not invited to every party or included by every crowd. It's good for children to have some close friends, but counterproductive for them to feel dependent on constant companionship.

kids think that if they have popular friends, they won't get picked on.

The most important thing to know is that a lot of the kids who get left out of the popular crowds, like you, may someday be more successful than the popular kids. What makes people successful in life isn't necessarily what makes them popular in school, and after high school nobody really cares if you were popular or not. I know it hurts right now, but you're talented in music and you're a very good student, and the popular kids only seem interested in partying. Your friends in orchestra and the kids who work hard in school are much more likely to get the good scholarships to colleges and find the best jobs. I'm so sorry you feel bad and I suppose my story doesn't help you feel better about things now, but your future can be much brighter because you're developing your talents. It really isn't important to have a lot of friends who don't have good intentions.

You have some really close friends—like Andy, Michael, and Abby—and they'll be there for you, even when other kids are mean.

Danielle: I guess you're right, but it's still hard. I think I'll go e-mail Abby. Those kids aren't mean to her, but at least I think she'll understand. Then maybe I'd better practice my cello for the concert next week.

COPING WITH THE CLOTHES CRISIS

Whether styles dictate tight stretch pants, tight tops, or exposed midriffs, overweight children, and especially overweight girls, are often stuck out of style. Chubby or plus-size clothes don't even attempt the styles that "in" brand names promote. Although adult clothing usually fits overweight teens better than teenage clothes do, it doesn't necessarily help kids fit in. The middle school boys in my focus groups were vocal and nasty about overweight girls' attempts to dress stylishly because their clothes often emphasized their overweight. The dress dilemma continues to be an unremitting pressure to overweight children. Arielle, a seventh-grader, found her own creative approach to coping with her fashion anxieties.

Arielle Solves Her Clothes Problem

Our family lives on a beef farm, and we also raise chickens. When Arielle was in fifth grade, she decided she never wanted to eat another animal again, so she became a vegetarian. But instead of eating the vegetables she claimed she'd eaten, she ate pasta, white bread, cakes, and other simple carbohydrates. Her body shape changed quickly, and she became very fat. By ninth grade she had also developed very large breasts. Normal clothes were hard to find, but Arielle wasn't interested in brand names. She was determined that her clothes would be original and unique. She shopped at Goodwill and Salvation Army thrift shops to put together outfits from times past. This brought her plenty of attention, which I suppose was Arielle's way of coping with not being able to fit into the fashionable clothes that her peers wore. She masked her desperation with unique attire.

Arielle's mother

Parents may not be able to assist children with the clothes struggle as much as they'd like, but being empathic about the problem will at least provide some support. For instance, you can be patient while shopping with your overweight child since it may take longer to find him outfits that fit appropriately. You can also help him find styles that are attractive for his size, whether or not the clothes have brand names, and sometimes you may even find the "right" brand names in plus sizes. Searching the Internet for plus-size clothes is also another possible option. If you're talented enough to sew properly fitting clothes for your overweight child, it's worth your time to make the special effort. Recall when Terri's mom sewed her a dress and made her feel "like a million bucks"? Terri never forgot her mother's special effort, and your children will remember yours.

Although parents should also remind their children of all their other good qualities and try to convince them that they are more than just their appearances, all children like to feel they can look nice. If your child is donning huge, ugly shirts to cover her embarrassing figure, tell her you understand her concerns, and then help her find reasonable clothes that will cover her comfortably and attractively. Even if you're anxious for your child, be sure to tell her, "You look good (or cool)," before she leaves for a party, or remind her of her good personality or terrific sense of humor. She'll be able to reflect on your compliments when she spontaneously compares herself with thinner or more stylishly dressed peers. Hopefully, she'll be busy chatting and laughing with her friends instead of thinking only about her clothes and worrying about being fat.

LEARNING RESILIENCE AND OPTIMISM

The independence and resilience demanded of overweight children goes far beyond the expectations for normal-weight children. Many of their peers don't accept them, as illustrated above, and as I'll show in upcoming chapters, even adults, parents, and teachers are less accepting. So it's critical that we as parents teach our children qualities of resilience and optimism to help reverse their pessimism and worry.

Research shows that these qualities of resilience and optimism can make a dramatic difference in the lives of successful people. A long-term longitudinal study of economically, physically, and culturally deprived children in Hawaii found that despite the terrible disadvantages these children had, some emerged from their environments to earn college degrees and lead successful and happy lives. Researchers used the term resilience to describe the ability to persevere and optimistically move forward toward success despite incredible handicaps.

The *See Jane Win* research found that same optimism and resilience as characteristic of the more than 1,000 women included in the study. These women viewed problems as challenges they could overcome and had an I CAN attitude throughout their lives.

Research for *See Jane Win* also showed that optimism and resilience weren't necessarily typical of the entire family. Parents often describe their children as being "unhappy since birth," or to the contrary, "optimistic since birth." However, other parents recall with dismay how happy their children had been, but how their temperaments seemed to change dramatically after they entered middle or high school, college, or sometimes even adulthood—particularly if their children experienced dramatic weight gain.

With that in mind, here's what I suggest you do to help foster optimism and resilience in your middle schooler or teenager.

- *Believe in your children.* Assure your children you're on their side in their struggle to become the best people they can be, and although you expect them to do their best, you don't necessarily expect them to be *the* best at anything.
- *Find other adults who believe in your children.* Teachers, aunts, uncles, or scout or church leaders can help you to make a positive difference for your overweight children. If they can see beyond your children's overweight appearance to the talents and needs within, your children will feel better about themselves and take control of their lives to build the resilience they need to develop themselves into creative, productive, and healthy young people.
- *Encourage your children to stay interested in activities.* Let them know their interests are valued even if they're not involved in high-status activities. For example, your children may prefer to work backstage rather than perform on the stage. Being part of a school drama production is important, even if children aren't in a star role. Overweight children may be less willing to be on a stage in front of a large audience.
- *Be sensitive, but not oversensitive.* When you act as if you believe your children's negative experiences are disastrous, it may further convince them that they are failures. See "Brianna Has Her Own Sleepover" for an example of an appropriate response.
- *Celebrate your children's winning experiences and help them accept defeats graciously.* Let them know you appreciate their efforts and positive attitudes whether they win or lose. Their attitudes and efforts are more important than their victories.

BRIANNA HAS HER OWN SLEEPOVER

Brianna: (down in the dumps) Amanda's having a sleepover on Saturday and almost all the girls in the class were invited except for me.

Mom: That must feel pretty bad. Maybe Amanda's mom only let her invite a certain number of friends. Are there any of your friends who aren't going?

Brianna: Just a couple. Well, I guess maybe five or six other kids in the class weren't invited, but only a couple of my friends.

Mom: Would you want to invite one of your friends here for a sleepover? Maybe Kritchie's not going, and you two always have a good time together.

Brianna: That's a good idea. I hope she can come.

• *Point out good sportsmanship.* While watching amateur or professional sports, admire players who have positive attitudes. Also note your disappointment with players who show negative attitudes or behaviors.

• *Encourage upbeat conversations about your children's future.* Assume they are going on to college and thinking about good careers. Explain that they will find challenging and creative careers more interesting and rewarding. Let them know you believe they're capable.

• *Be a role model for perseverance.* Be sure your children hear you say that tasks are difficult, but that you're not a quitter.

• *Model an I CAN attitude.* Be reasonably optimistic and let your kids know you can succeed or will at least give an activity your best try.

• *Encourage family fun and laughter.* A family that can joke, laugh, and lighten up their days with humor can prevent children's believing that their lives will move in a negative direction. Family fun releases tension and helps children to feel optimistic about their future.

HANDLING PEER BULLIES

Even adolescents with good self-esteem may wither on the vine from continuous taunting and teasing by powerful, popular kids or obnoxious bullies. They will have to do more than just cry about the problem, although a few tears when they come home distressed are justifiable and should receive your support and an understanding hug.

Beyond comfort, your children will need some tools for coping that will hopefully diminish the problem. There is no easy way to stop taunting, but here are some approaches proven effective for other overweight children.

Find a Friend in Need

Teachers may be able to help overweight children by appointing them to tutor someone who needs help or to assist a child with disabilities. Not only will that help overweight children to be appreciative of their own abilities and their bodies, but it will help them to concentrate their energies on caring about others as well. The peer effect is likely to be good, as it was for Stuart, who became friends with a blind student in his class. You can't help but admire a kid who goes out of his way to help a person with a handicap.

Find a Peer Ally

Remember how Darlene talked to the girlfriends of the boys who were taunting her and they told their boyfriends to stop? If your child has a friend among the leaders of the class, having her privately tell that leader how much the teasing hurts is a good plan. Children will feel better if they communicate directly to a friend and are successful in saving themselves.

Discover an Activity Strength

A child who becomes a star of a sport, the drama club, or the math team soon finds allies. Teammates don't pick on one of their own if they want someone on their team, and bullies don't taunt kids when they're surrounded by friends who'll defend them. Remember how Matt found some security through football, and more through track? My research found that very few of the boys who were active in sports suffered much taunting.

Although not all overweight children can count on being team players in sports, interests in speech, drama, or band can also offer opportunities for overweight children to discover pockets of support in and out of school. When your overweight child sings a solo or receives a trophy for math or wrestling, the peer taunting diminishes a little and the admiration grows slightly. Every little bit helps.

Stop the Teasing

Children who taunt and insult others aren't necessarily mean children. They may not realize that they're hurting others. Adults, like teachers, can take leaders aside, appeal to their sensitive sides, and get them to stop the teasing. Adults should take care to communicate such concerns privately, however; discussing the matter in front of peers could embarrass the leader and unleash the leader's power to taunt even more. This tactic may be more effective with girls than boys, but it's worth trying for both. Here are ways your child can counteract teasing.

- *Learn a sharp response.* A sharp response pointing out a taunter's weaknesses may incite fear in a taunter, which will eradicate any further slurs. "Haven't you learned your multiplication facts yet?" or "You're so small I could put you in my back pocket" or "My 6-foot brother is on the football team, and he doesn't like it when little squirts like you call me names" or "I consider that a compliment, coming from you" seemed to be effective for some of the adult interviewees when they were overweight as kids. You'll have to determine your child's own courage level before you recommend she try to thwart bullies with a mean comment. That kind of response can backfire, and when children fear that their taunters may take them on physically, a smart response will probably not be effective. It may be better for such children to ignore the taunts and then find a friend to play with or a teacher to talk to in order to gain protection from the bullies.
- *Scowl in disdain.* Being very large and overweight does not protect other kids from taunting, but it can give some advantage in defense. A scowl may intimidate better than words, and while big kids might rather

just be friends, an angry frown can be effective in threatening popular small kids who are trying to make a scene.

- **Keep emotions under control.** Adults might think that if overweight kids cry when they are teased, peers will be more likely to realize how much the teasing hurts and be nicer to those kids. Unfortunately, bullies see tears as weak, stupid, silly, and babyish and assume "this wimp of a kid" needs a lesson, which they deliver mercilessly. If kids lose their temper when taunted, that rarely helps either. It's hard for kids to walk away when they're angry, but that may be the best alternative. If children can't control their emotions in front of peers, the situation might require some adult intervention. Here are some suggestions to offer your child.

- Try to control the tears or anger until you're at home so that the bullies don't have another reason to tease you.
- Walk away, ignore the taunts, and tell yourself, "Don't cry, don't cry."
- Change the tears to laughter, or make a joke and disarm the crowd while also relieving some of your own tension.
- Find a close friend who will support you, and walk as far away as possible.
- Talk privately to a teacher or principal who is in a powerful position to change the bullying behavior by speaking with your class or group.

Contact an Authority

If your child feels threatened, it may be necessary for you to report the problem to the appropriate authorities. Furthermore, even if your child is afraid to be called a tattler, you may have to encourage him to report serious threats to an authority immediately. Explain that there's a difference between tattling and reporting. Tattlers tell authorities just to get another person into trouble, and they're not really worried about the consequences for themselves or others. However, if children believe they or others might not be safe, it's always appropriate to report the situation to an authority figure who can provide protection, and that kind of reporting is definitely *not* tattling. Reporting problems to authorities can prevent disasters.

Eighth-grader Matt reported he actually had fears that bullies who also hunted with their dads had access to guns and might use them on him if provoked. I encouraged Matt to be sure to report his concerns to his parents and the principal if he was ever actually threatened with a gun, and I encourage parents and teachers to report threats to the police if appropriate.

In order for my last suggestions to be effective, an authority will need to investigate and label taunting as "bullying" behavior, state that bullying behavior isn't accepted at the school or program, and make that statement not only for a specific child but for any child called "fat" or "dumb" or belittled in other inappropriate ways. If the school follows through by requiring a visit to the principal's office, a conference with the parents, or an appropriate punishment, the bullying will diminish and children will be safe from the worst taunting. That will not prevent the occasional individual insults that are less obvious, but children can manage to ignore them and walk away to eventually dissipate those.

Reassure Your Child

Your child deserves reassurance that he is a good, smart, and effective person despite what others may say or do. He also needs to know how to cope effectively by not playing the victim. You should be supportive of his feelings, but don't host a daily pity party—with or without food. It's not helpful to your child to allow him to dwell in self-pity. Sometimes children learn they can get plenty of attention from a parent when they describe how mean others are. Of course, they truly are hurt, but they need advice that will move them forward to their interests and strengths. Helping your child to develop his personal strengths can guide him toward positive accomplishments that will build his self-esteem.

DEALING WITH DEPRESSION

If your child feels depressed, you should have her evaluated by a psychologist. Depression can be a serious problem and should not be ignored or dismissed. The following symptoms of depression should alert you to seek professional help.

• Excessive sleeping
• Having difficulty waking in the morning
• Complaining of stomachaches or headaches
• Withdrawing from social activities
• Declining grades
• Frequent snacking

When children are anxious and depressed, they may indeed be motivated to ease their depression with foods rich in simple carbohydrates. Carbohydrates temporarily boost serotonin levels and calm and soothe sad
feelings. Unfortunately, these foods don't solve the problems of heavy children, and instead add to their weight difficulties. Nutrition expert Elizabeth
Somer, a registered dietitian and the author of *Food and Mood: The Complete Guide to Eating Well and Feeling Your Best*, recommends snacks rich
in vitamins and complex carbs that are also low in calories, such as fresh
fruit, popcorn, or raw veggies with low-fat dip, to take the place of problem
foods like ice cream, doughnuts, and cookies. Changing eating habits is
only part of the solution, though.

CHAPTER 4

THE ACADEMIC DIFFERENCE:
How Being Overweight Affects School Achievement

T he previous chapter's findings paint a vivid picture of the social challenges that our overweight children face. When it comes to academic achievement, however, one would expect a more level playing field. In the classroom, we expect all children to be treated equally and with equal opportunity for success.

Astoundingly, this is not the case.

There is no apparent reason that being overweight should influence intellectual accomplishments. We would expect that intelligence should be normally distributed among children of all weight categories, and that school achievement should also follow that normal distribution. And in fact, given chapter 3's explanation of the lack of social opportunities for overweight kids, it would be reasonable to even expect some gains among the group as they focus on intellectual pursuits rather than physical activities or climbing the social ladder. And yet, we found the opposite to be true: The classroom is no more of a safe haven for our overweight children than is the social scene.

Every school day, overweight students are faced with difficult relationships with their teachers, the likelihood of placement in special programs, and the stigma of being considered lazy.

PART 1—THE FINDINGS

Across almost every variable and measure of academic performance and optimism in our survey, very overweight kids trail their peers.

- A smaller percentage of very overweight children are enrolled in gifted and talented programs.
- Very overweight children are twice as likely to be enrolled in special programs for attention deficit disorders (ADD), 33 percent more likely to be treated for learning disabilities, and three times as likely to be placed in special programs for behavioral or emotional disabilities than average-weight kids.
- Overweight and very overweight children are less likely to describe themselves as smart, talented, or gifted, even when they are enrolled in gifted programming.
- Compared with average-weight children, overweight and very overweight children are less likely to describe themselves as hard workers and twice as likely to see themselves as lazy. This is despite the fact that overweight kids reported investing more time in homework than average-weight kids did.
- Overweight children are much more likely than average-weight children to report that their teachers don't understand them.

While it's clear that overweight children start from lower self-image perspectives than their peers, parents and educators can help these children recognize their intelligence and unique skills in ways that can raise their academic confidence, work ethic, and achievement levels. In order to accomplish this transformation, we need to first understand how weight is affecting our children's academic underachievement.

FEELING SMART

No matter how well overweight children perform in school, there is a good chance that they will not see themselves as gifted, talented, or smart. While

Figure 4.1
Self-Description of Intelligence, by Weight Category

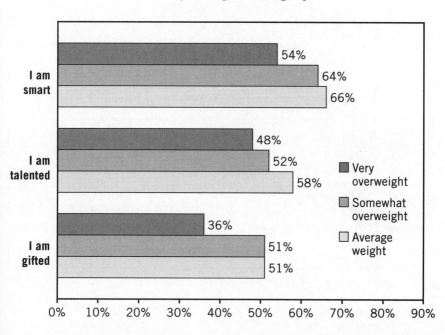

just under half (48 percent) of the very overweight children credited themselves as being talented, 58 percent of the average-weight children labeled themselves as talented (see figure 4.1). Perception of weight also was associated with whether these children thought of themselves as smart (54 percent for very overweight children, compared with 64 percent for somewhat overweight and 66 percent for average-weight children). Completing this dismal picture of the children's judgments of their own skills and aptitudes is the finding that overweight children have a lower perception of both their grades and their intelligence (see figures 4.2 and 4.3 on pages 80 and 81).

The relationship between children's weight and their optimism about their own intelligence is also demonstrated by the comparison of actual enrollment of children in gifted programs in association with the children's perceptions of themselves. Even though the differences in actual enrollment

Figure 4.2
Self-Description of Grades in School, by Weight Category

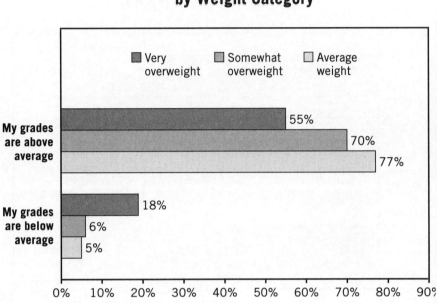

in gifted programs among overweight and other children were relatively small (see figure 4.4 on page 83), there was a vast and startling contrast in how the different categories of children described themselves.

Figure 4.1 shows how much children's perceptions of their weight affected their descriptions of their abilities. More than half (51 percent) of the average-weight kids and somewhat overweight kids rated themselves as gifted, compared with only 36 percent of the very overweight kids. The numbers speak to the natural optimism that average-weight and somewhat overweight kids have that their very overweight peers do not share. While only 41 percent of somewhat overweight or average-weight kids were enrolled in gifted programs, a full 51 percent described themselves as gifted. This contrasts with very overweight kids, who seemed to have a much narrower view of their gifts: 35 percent of them were enrolled in gifted programs, and 36 percent of them described themselves as gifted.

Figure 4.3
Self-Perception of Intelligence, by Weight Category

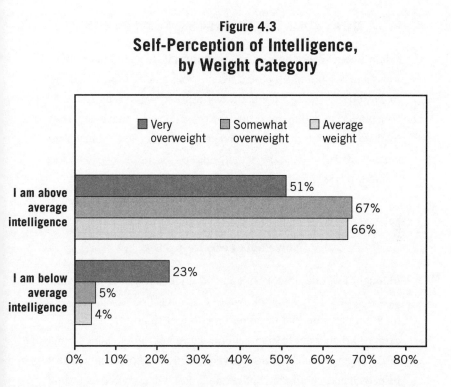

Self-Perceptions of Intelligence

Very few of the adults interviewed considered themselves smart when they were younger, although most were college graduates and all felt intelligent as adults. Astonishing were the examples of interviewees who, when they were clearly among the best and brightest of their classes, never believed they were smart.

Nancy Was Gifted, but Didn't Believe

I was a pretty smart kid, in the gifted program and advanced place-ment classes, and I went to the Air Force Academy for college. Nevertheless, I never considered myself smart despite those high achievements. I simply had low self-esteem.

Nancy, adult interviewee

Darlene Didn't Feel Smart—She Felt like a Blob

I didn't believe anything good about myself, so I couldn't believe I was smart. I felt like a blob. I had terrible grades. I didn't believe in myself, so I didn't try hard. My attitude was "Why bother?" When I was in eighth grade, they gave us IQ and achievement tests to place us in high school. My dad got the report and he said, "Your teacher said you have the second-highest IQ in the class." I was floored. It was the first time I realized I might be really smart.

Darlene, adult interviewee

Now Paula Feels Respected

I thought I was dumb. I wasn't a good student. My best years came in a vocational high school, where I was enrolled in a health care dietitian program that permitted me to feel smarter and more accepted. I then went to chef school, was a very good student, and made lots of friends. As a supervisor in my workplace now, I feel respected and intelligent, but certainly not when I was overweight during adolescence.

Paula, adult interviewee

The Value of Feeling Smart and Being Considered Smart by Others

Making matters worse, the very overweight kids have turned these perceptions into conclusions about themselves that can lead them to believe that others believe the same way about them. They were more than twice as likely as average-weight kids to agree with the statement "I am not smart enough," and nearly twice as likely to report "My teachers don't understand me." (See figure 4.5 on page 84.)

The reason for these negative self-perceptions must be related to reflections of what other people believe about overweight children. The stereotypes related to overweight are as destructive as racial stereotypes. Adults and children alike immediately assume that fat children are dumb

Figure 4.4
Placement in School Special Education Programs, by Weight Category

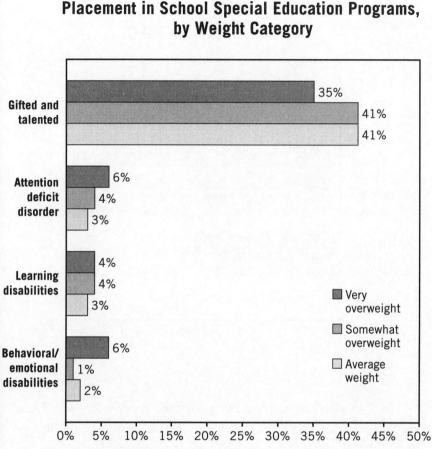

and lazy and that making insulting comments to that effect may convince overweight children that they cannot achieve beyond such low expectations.

Yet some of the adults interviewed felt smart from the start despite their weight, and others gained confidence in their intelligence through hard work. Harry's parents and older siblings assured him that knowing his multiplication facts was more important than being king of the playground if he was going on to college, which he always planned on doing. That's a goal that almost all parents can set for their children.

Figure 4.5
Worries about Academic Issues, by Weight Category

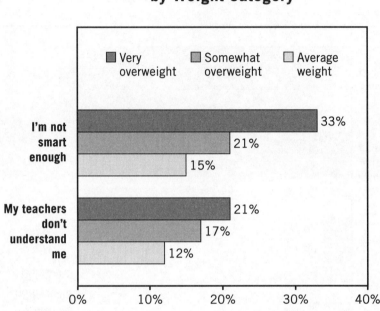

Terri, an adult interviewee, actually felt smart in elementary school, but she was not placed in honors classes in middle school. She worked very hard, and gradually, one class at a time, she moved into the higher track. By high school she was in mostly honors classes. Terri's family members were staunch supporters of her intelligence. In retrospect, Terri realized that when she went into a new and larger school environment, other kids alienated her because of her overweight. However, once they discovered she was smart and friendly, she was accepted despite her weight. Children's weight may at first set negative expectations, but once they have a reputation for being intelligent, their weight will not change their reputations among those who already know them.

An underachiever in middle and high schools, Lorie didn't find out until college that she could establish a reputation as an A student. Once she did well in her first semester, her professors and college peers assumed she was intelligent and treated her that way.

Why Feeling Smart Is So Important

Considerable research data proves that academic success is the best predictor of career success. Students who get good grades are more likely to continue their education beyond high school and are more likely to be employed in the most rewarding jobs. In order for children to be successful academically, they should also feel reasonably intelligent, so the wish to be and feel smart is strongly ingrained in American culture.

Being too smart in the middle school culture is, however, a mixed blessing. Middle school children tend to admire intelligent kids as long as they play sports, are good-looking and cool, and don't work too hard. But if smart kids are too conscientious or serious or aren't as attractive, they quickly fall out of the popular crowd. Thus, middle school kids often feel torn. On one hand, they want to get good grades to please their parents, teachers, and themselves. On the other hand, if they seem too serious about their learning, they pay a social price.

Harry used his intelligence to defeat the teasing crowd on the playground. At the root of his successful behavior was his academic self-confidence, which he attributes to family influence. His smarts did not necessarily make him popular, but his quick responses let him protect himself from playground bullies.

Harry's Success Story from the School Yard

I was the last kid on the playground picked for soccer at recess, and some kids would taunt me and say, "You're slow because you're so fat." I had a sharp tongue and I could retort: "But I know my multiplication tables through 14 and you don't. So there!" My older brother was in college by the time I was in fourth grade. He would tell me it didn't really matter who was king of the playground if you were going to college.

Harry, adult interviewee

UNDERACHIEVEMENT

Many of the adults interviewed described their childhood underachievement problems. Patti, better known as Fatty Patti, claimed she was a dreamer and didn't apply herself. The teachers assumed she was shy and quiet and they never expected much from her. Ralph considered himself a decent B student, but applied himself in only math and technical drawing—the subjects he loved. He earned A's in those subjects and is an engineer today.

Underachievement is a term used to describe children who are not working up to their abilities in school. For some it means being placed in special education classes instead of the regular track, and for others it results in being placed in the regular track rather than honors courses. The causes for underachievement for overweight children may be a direct result of their emotional trauma, which in turn influences self-image, work ethic, and study habits as well as physical factors affecting their concentration. Overweight children shunned or insulted by adults and other children may feel so discouraged that they may lose confidence in all areas of their lives.

Underachievement and overeating share psychological similarities. That is, both are a group of defense mechanisms that indicate feelings of discouragement. Children avoid doing schoolwork because they believe that even if they put forth appropriate effort, it will not result in good grades or teacher or parental approval. They protect their fragile self-concepts by making excuses, blaming teachers or parents, or claiming schoolwork is boring. Underachieving by not accomplishing homework or by not studying becomes a bad habit, and grades become worse, thus causing these children to lose even more of their academic confidence. They often say they don't care, but maybe they dream of magically becoming valedictorian.

Similarly, overeating and underexercising represent children's beliefs that even if they eat less and exercise more, they will not succeed in being attractive, healthy, or thin. Therefore, they may as well enjoy their food and television as solace for what they believe they can't accomplish anyway. As overweight children make excuses and deny they have a problem, they convince themselves that there is nothing they can do to become healthier. Often, they may say they don't care, but they may dream they can become thin and beautiful through some magical power. They realize there is a societal advantage in physical beauty; they simply have no hope of achieving it.

Behavioral and Emotional Disabilities

When it came to placement in special school programs, overweight kids were more likely to be enrolled in classes for attention deficit disorder, learning disabilities, and behavioral and emotional disabilities. The largest differences among weight groups appeared in the behavioral and emotional disabilities classrooms, with three times the percentage of very overweight children in these special classes (see figure 4.4 on page 83). No doubt the emotional abuse by peers and the prejudice toward obese children by both children and adults contributed to this very striking discovery.

When children are taunted continuously or isolated from friendships, they may seek attention in negative and antisocial ways. An 8-year study of almost 1,000 children, conducted by Sarah Mustillo, Ph.D., of Duke University Medical Center in Durham, North Carolina, found that children who were chronically obese were more likely to suffer from psychiatric disorders, including oppositional defiant disorder and depression. Children diagnosed with oppositional defiant disorder behave in a rebellious manner, determined to oppose whatever adults suggest. This, of course, causes serious problems both at home and in school. And obese children who are depressed or anxious will not be able to function well in a regular classroom.

Among the adult interviewees, none had qualified for special education classes because there were few of these offered while they were growing up. Yet many of the adults I spoke to admitted to having struggled with shyness, poor concentration, isolation, and truancy.

Schools classify children with emotional disturbances because they can then provide children with special services to help them with their struggles. Doreen's daughter received the help she needed and will soon return to regular classes, hopefully with renewed confidence (see "Doreen: A Mother's Worries" on page 89).

When fat children are considered dumb or are ostracized by being placed in special education or emotional disabilities classes, this can strongly affect their self-confidence. Once they no longer believe in their

Figure 4.6
Self-Description of Work Ethic, by Weight Category

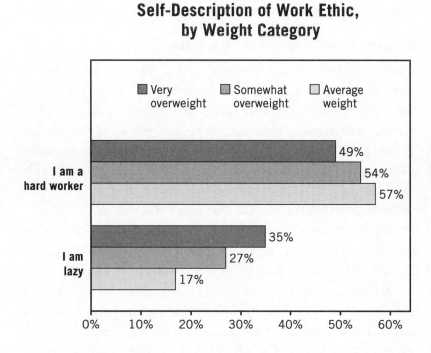

abilities to achieve, it's unlikely they will work hard, or, like Ralph, they may work hard only in the few areas where they have complete confidence.

A WORK ETHIC

Figure 4.6 shows that overweight children were less likely to think of themselves as hard workers (49 percent and 54 percent, compared with 57 percent) and more likely to describe themselves as lazy (35 percent and 27 percent, compared with 17 percent). The smaller percentage of overweight children who indicated they were hard workers and the higher percentage of those who described themselves as lazy may confirm that there is more underachievement among overweight children.

This is an important area where parents can intervene to help establish

DOREEN: A MOTHER'S WORRIES

Doreen shared her own painful story of being overweight, as well as those of her three daughters.

Her oldest and youngest daughters were A students, and although they were somewhat tall and large-boned, neither was obese. The middle daughter, the most overweight of the three, struggled with reading and was a poor student and an underachiever. She was also in a special intervention program for children with emotional problems because she had brought unidentified pills to school. Her close friend had threatened suicide, and rather than tell an adult, she kept the secret to herself for her friend's protection. She then brought pills to school to show her friend that she would kill herself if her friend did the same. She claimed she had hoped to prevent her friend's suicide by her own threat and that she had not really planned to harm herself. It was this incident that placed her in the special intervention program.

Doreen believed that because her daughter was fat, she felt needy for friendship and would do almost anything to hold on to friends. Doreen worried as she watched her daughter continuously gain more weight, and she wondered, *Is it the overweight that alienates friends? Is it the poor grades and underachievement that rupture friendships? Or is it the lack of friends and poor achievement that motivate the continuous eating?* Even though the root cause is difficult to pin down, the effect of this cycle of emotional upheaval has clearly taken its toll on Doreen's daughter.

and appreciate a stronger work ethic for their children. For adult interviewees Nina, Sandra, Terri, and Jeff, the development of a work ethic was important to their success. Nina figured she was a good student only because she didn't have much else to focus on. She didn't have a social life and would sit at home, do her schoolwork, watch television, or do needlepoint. Her mother considered taking her to a psychologist because "sitting at home" was Nina's only interest. Sandra also considered herself an excellent student, but she admitted that school and learning were a refuge, and at least she felt good about her school achievement.

Terri, another good student, believed she'd been wrongly placed in a regular academic track and worked hard to move to the honors track. In middle school, she didn't feel connected to other students, and as a result she ate more. She found herself crying every other day, but by working hard in school, she was gradually placed in more honors classes. By ninth grade she had lost 20 pounds and she was in honors classes. However, Terri didn't attribute her weight loss to her change in class status. It is possible that earlier poor work habits or unconscious teacher prejudice initially placed her in the wrong track, but Terri will never know for sure. By high school she was at an excellent weight and was an excellent student; she went on to college success.

Jeff was dyslexic before most schools understood reading disability problems. Now in his forties, Jeff is very successful, thanks to the winning combination of his effervescent personality and his computer skills. He attributes the development of his work ethic and much of his self-confidence to his childhood work experience in his parents' clothing store.

Jeff Learned to Work Hard

I never thought of myself as overly intelligent. I believed that it was hard work that would get me through. I tried to stay focused and driven, but I never read for pleasure because it was such a struggle. If I had to put my hand to paper, I just couldn't write. Handwriting, spelling, and grammar baffled me, and no matter how much I was tutored and helped with them, they were always struggles for me. I would freeze up, and my thoughts were paralyzed, too. If not for the computer and spell check, I'd never write now. I can write creatively and well, as long as I have a computer.

Jeff, adult interviewee

More Time on Homework, without the Payoff

Despite not always perceiving themselves as hard workers, very overweight children indicated they actually spent more time on homework (an average of 2.1 hours daily) than did somewhat overweight and average-weight children (1.7 and 1.5 hours respectively). (See figure 4.7 on page 92.) So why would children who work longer not view themselves as hard workers and instead think of themselves as lazy?

Talking to adults who were overweight as children points to the persistent stereotype that overweight is equated with being lazy. The children's perceptions that they were lazy seem to be related more to being *labeled* as lazy by others than to the actual effort they set forth. What's more, for the adults like Sandra and Terri, the reason they studied more as kids was because they had fewer friends to spend time with. The sadness of this social situation may also interfere with overweight children's powers of concentration and efficiency in studying. As a result, it can take children who lack social confidence more time to accomplish similar quantities of work. Because they find food so comforting, they may take more snack breaks. So they spend more time but don't actually get any further ahead. That only causes them to become more discouraged about their ability to achieve and feel smart.

Poor Nutrition

In addition to low self-esteem, social problems, and a lower perceived work ethic, there may be physical factors affecting overweight kids' academic performance. Poor nutrition and insufficient exercise may dramatically diminish thinking and concentrating skills. It's typically assumed that overweight children have plenty of nourishment, but they may actually be undernourished despite the quantities of calories they consume. Daniel Amen, M.D., a child and adult psychiatrist and medical director of The Amen Clinics in Newport Beach and Fairfield, California, and Tacoma, Washington, points out that most children breakfast on simple carbohydrates like muffins, doughnuts, bagels, or sugary cereals, which not only zap energy but diminish children's attention. Instead, he recommends a protein for breakfast—such as cheese, lean meat, or eggs—which will enhance energy and concentration and most likely improve kids' performance at school. Furthermore, a study of 5,400 school-age children published in the journal *Pediatrics* showed that iron deficiency, which

Figure 4.7
Average Time Spent on Homework,
by Weight Category

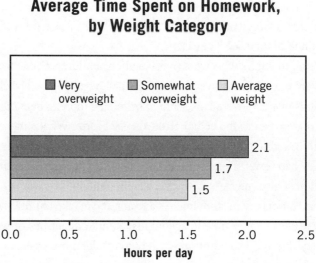

was most frequently a problem for adolescent girls, decreased children's attention and lowered their scores on standardized tests of mental development. It also had a significant impact on their performance on math exams.

Karen Collins, a registered dietitian and nutrition education consultant for the American Institute for Cancer Research in Washington, D.C., also explains why eating sweets is counterproductive to learning. It causes a surge of energy, followed by a drop in blood sugar, which then leaves children feeling tired. Collins maintains that children who consume nutrition bars or caffeinated soft drinks may also have trouble sitting still or concentrating because caffeine and carbohydrates cause children to feel overstimulated and restless.

And some overweight kids skip meals, like Sally, who as a kid used to go to the art room rather than eat lunch with her peers because she feared embarrassment. Missing meals does not provide children with the energy needed for learning.

Finally there's also evidence that children who are fat but not fit will have lower energy levels, and thus (wrongly) be perceived as lazy, which can start the cycle that leads to underachievement.

THE EFFECT OF SOCIAL CONFIDENCE AND ACCEPTANCE ON ACADEMIC PERFORMANCE

Some dramatic examples of how the lack of social self-confidence can spill over to school performance were obvious in Gabi's and Sally's tendencies to "act out." Both of them found acceptance only in very "wrong" peer groups as kids, and that had a great negative effect on their school performance.

Gabi's Parents to the Rescue

I started using drugs in seventh grade—like smoking pot, and dealing and selling pills—and getting in with the wrong kids. Weight wasn't an issue with these kids. They accepted me for just being in the drug scene and weren't concerned about my being fat. The fact that I skipped school was finally brought to my parents' attention when I was absent for 30 days in a row in 10th grade. My parents put me in drug rehabilitation and then had me transferred to a new school. I had to account for every minute of every day, and I hated the restriction. In rehab I learned a lot about relationships, instead of just focusing my life on getting money for drugs. I appreciate what my parents did now, although I didn't at the time. I put my act together in 11th grade at my new school, earned good grades, and went on to be successful in college and in my career. I also took control of my weight in 11th grade, and that helped make a huge difference for me.

Gabi, adult interviewee

Sally Finally Saved Herself

I didn't feel like I was socially smart, and I felt like an outcast. I hung out with the kids who were on drugs and were troublemakers. I would skip classes and still get passing grades, so I knew I was intelligent enough to slide through. The school finally called my parents and said I had missed 50 days of school, but my parents hadn't realized until then that I'd been absent. I dropped out of school, married the wrong person, and divorced soon afterward. I ended up getting my GED and finally took control of my life. I went to college, and I now have a successful career and a healthy lifestyle.

Sally, adult interviewee

Teachers' Attitudes toward Overweight Students

It's not just peer attitudes that adversely affect children's perceptions of their talents and intelligence, but teachers' attitudes as well. As mentioned earlier in the chapter and shown in figure 4.5 on page 84, children who perceived themselves as very overweight and somewhat overweight were more likely to believe that their teachers didn't understand them. Only 12 percent of the average-weight students, compared with 17 percent of the somewhat overweight students and a full 21 percent of the very overweight students, indicated that they worried about that issue quite a lot. Overweight children's worries may have been directly related to some teachers' lack of empathy for them, or if these children were underachieving, they might have blamed teachers for their problems.

Although most adults interviewed felt that their teachers were fair, very few talked about inspirational teachers who had made special efforts to help them. Lorie's story of her inspirational teacher was an exception. Lorie was an underachieving student and never considered herself smart in middle school. Then in high school her French teacher told Lorie she was smart, and she began getting better grades in French. Lorie was introduced to her teacher's husband as "her number-one student," and that gave Lorie some confidence for going on to college, where she excelled.

On the other hand, Phyllis's gym teacher seemed to do more harm than good. The gym teacher tried to help by calling Phyllis's mom to explain that Phyllis was obese and needed to lose weight. Her mother's response— "Thanks for telling me that, but she'll take care of herself"— wasn't helpful to Phyllis. To this day, Phyllis claims she still hates that teacher. She explains that although it was obvious the teacher was trying to be helpful, the woman's call rubbed her the wrong way. Perhaps if Phyllis's mother had interpreted the teacher's comments differently, Phyllis might have been able to see those comments as helpful. Phyllis's teacher was kind for trying to help her, but because of the response she received, I'm not sure that teacher would have dared to warn another parent about a weight problem.

Amanda's basketball coach handled the weight concern differently, and that conversation was very helpful to Amanda.

A Coach Reaches Amanda

One of my high school basketball coaches made a difference for me. I was a sophomore in high school and after practice one day my coach said, "Come into my office. I'd like to talk to you." I went in and he was very tactful and diplomatic. He said, "You're really good and you're going to be a great asset to this team, and junior-senior year you're going to be playing a lot. I think you should think about losing a little weight—if for no other reason than basketball. I think you'd be a lot faster and better if you lost just a little weight." He added, "Obviously it's good for you health-wise and a lot of other reasons, but I'd like to suggest it for basketball."

I think he probably thought it would just be good for me and maybe basketball was a way to convince me because I was so dedicated to the sport. It concerned me. In high school, we had the option of eating the cafeteria food or selecting from the salad bar. I remember thinking about it, and I started eating salads for lunch instead of the cafeteria food, which was horrible and high in fat. About a month later my dad said, "I was watching you on the basketball court. I think you've lost a little bit of weight." I wasn't really aware that I had lost weight, but I guess my dad noticed. I had lost 10 pounds. I hadn't really thought about wanting to get smaller, but became suddenly aware of "huh . . . my basketball uniform is baggier now." My coach really helped.

Amanda, adult interviewee

Notice the commonality of these stories. When teachers were able to focus on students' strengths and develop an alliance, they enabled students to do something about their problems. Although teachers didn't necessarily have a direct effect on immediate school performance, we can assume that if they encouraged overweight kids to take control of their health, the students' improved health would also foster better academic success. If the teacher only pointed out faults, the student became defensive and angry and did not take advice from that teacher.

The negative stories about teachers were, unfortunately, more frequent than the positive stories. Many teachers made insulting comments to students who were overweight. Paula's sixth-grade teacher asked the class what kind of exercise they did. Paula raised her hand and answered, "Horseback riding." Her teacher responded, "That's only exercise if you carry the horse." It's easy to imagine how embarrassed Paula felt.

Ralph's seventh-grade teacher wasn't much better. Ralph remembered fooling around in science class, and his science teacher called him El Blimpo in front of the whole class. Ralph was more shocked than embarrassed and came home and repeated the story to his parents. They phoned the school, and the teacher never called him El Blimpo again. Ralph said that he wishes he could see that teacher again, just so he could show off his strong, slim adult physique.

Likewise, Sally found herself scheduled for a double science period during what was normally her lunch period, so she innocently asked the science teacher when she would be able to eat lunch. He stared at her overweight body and answered—in front of the class—"It doesn't look like you need to go to lunch." Incidentally, Sally said that the science teacher probably weighed 250 pounds, but his own overweight apparently had little impact on his empathy.

TWO PATHS EMERGE: CONTRASTING EFFECTS ON ACHIEVEMENT

There seem to be two opposite directions that overweight children take in school. The more frequent direction seems to be that children's overall self-esteem generalizes to their academic self-confidence and thus causes them to underachieve and feel less capable than they are. The alternative, less common path is that they manage to feel smart and work hard at school because they either love to learn or find learning a shelter from a peer world that doesn't accept them. In the same manner that overweight girls are often told they have pretty faces, which implies that their bodies are not so pretty, some of the adult interviewees were told, "You have a great brain," which also implies that their bodies didn't measure up. That backhanded compliment led some of the overweight children to concentrate on their only apparent strength—their intelligence.

Lorie's underachievement pattern is a fairly typical one for girls whether overweight or not, but Lorie believed that her underachievement was a direct result of her being overweight.

A Future Valedictorian

I was an excellent student in elementary school, but in middle school I became focused on boys. I didn't have any interests or hobbies, so I just thought about how to attract boys. I was very competitive and didn't want to do things unless I was the best. I dropped out of dance, gymnastics, and basketball, and then I dropped out of doing schoolwork and deferred to television and eating. I felt that everyone thought I was fat.

I focused only on boyfriends, and what really got me losing weight was that a boy I had a crush on thought I was fat. I joined a gym and started counting fat grams. The boy didn't even like me, but I became dedicated to losing weight to prove I wasn't fat. The wish to prove something to a boy happened again when I was in college. I had an ex-boyfriend from high school who had cheated on me, and that made me feel really stupid. I felt like I had to prove to that guy that I was smart, so I started working hard in college. I got straight A's the first semester, so the professors considered me smart. I thought, Maybe I can do it again, and so I kept getting all A's and graduated from college as valedictorian of my class. My need to prove I wasn't dumb turned into a positive success story for me.

Lorie, adult interviewee

Obviously, if Lorie was able to be valedictorian of her college class, she could have earned good grades all through school. It was her being overweight that contributed dramatically to her loss of confidence in her intelligence. Her lack of intellectual self-confidence was directly tied to her nonacceptance by boys because she was fat. Some adults assume that non-acceptance by boys cannot matter that much, but for middle and high school girls today, a boyfriend is too often the only key to their self-confidence and achievement.

Lorie reversed her underachievement in college, but many under-achievers do not. Being overweight typically leads to lifelong under-achievement, which could be reversed if parents and teachers understood the special pressures that overweight children cope with.

PART II — RESCUING TECHNIQUES

Successful school achievement and feeling intelligent are important for your children's eventual fulfillment in life. As you encourage your child toward a healthy weight, you can prevent his weight problems from cheating him out of the psychological rewards of successful educational achievement. This section will guide you to:

- Help your child recognize her intelligence
- Teach your child a work ethic
- Help your child adjust to a new school environment
- Take an interest and share in your child's learning

• Communicate with your child's teachers
• Encourage healthy nutrition, which fosters learning
• Ensure that your child takes the path to achievement

HELPING YOUR CHILD RECOGNIZE HER INTELLIGENCE

The praise techniques from chapter 3 for helping children believe they are good people, attractive and personable, are also effective for helping children feel smart. When we praise children or allow them to hear us praise their qualities to others (referential talk) by referring to them as smart, intelligent, bright, talented, creative, clever, good thinkers, or hard workers, children tend to live up to those descriptions. Telling children they are stupid, bored, dumb, turned off by school, disorganized, not too sharp, or slow may cause them to underachieve or lose confidence in their abilities. That may seem obvious, but it's easy to get frustrated with children who don't put forth effort in school and slip into reinforcing that image with negative labels. Furthermore, those negative words may slip out when you're talking to teachers or other adults about your children. Children always seem to be listening whenever their name is mentioned.

Extreme praise and referential talk that includes words like "brilliant," "genius," "smartest," "perfect," and "most gifted" may motivate children to work very hard at first. However, these extremes may backfire, causing children to feel intense pressure when their school accomplishments fall short of what they assume are their parents' impossible standards. Very few children can live up to being the smartest, especially as children move into larger and more competitive schools. Being smartest becomes less attainable in older grades, while being a smart, good, or even excellent student continues to be very possible as long as children are willing to work hard.

When children are young, it's good to encourage them to think of fulfilling high-level careers and teach them to put aside some of their birthday money for their college funds, thus making the assumption early that of course they will go on to college. Whether your child chooses to be a firefighter, a doctor, or a teacher, explain that careers are important and that excelling in school will help her achieve her goals.

TEACHING YOUR CHILD A WORK ETHIC

Children will continue to feel smart in school only if they develop a work ethic. That is, bright children in younger grades can often feel smart with little effort because the curriculum is less difficult, but as they encounter a more challenging curriculum in middle school, their confidence in their intelligence will dissipate if they don't learn to work hard. You will recall from earlier in this chapter that children who wish to be smart without working hard often become underachievers and lose confidence in their intelligence. Pairing intelligence with hard work will ensure that children continue to feel smart. It's good to tell children that *the harder they work, the smarter they are, and the smarter they are, the harder they'll work.*

Teaching your child a work ethic for schoolwork as well as other kinds of work will make a big difference in his confidence, intelligence, and overall self-esteem. Here are some important ways to do this.

- *Praise your child as a hard worker when you observe him making strong efforts.* His efforts may be in schoolwork, housework or chores, yard work, or volunteering in the community. Praising him with compliments like "You persevere," "You're not a quitter," "You make a difference," or "I can count on you" will make your child value his hardworking capabilities.
- *Refer to your child's positive efforts in referential talk with other adults.* Parents seem even more believable to children when children hear them talking to other adults. Children never fail to listen when they hear you talking about them. Saying, "She's such a great help," "She's so responsible," "She accomplishes so much," or "She doesn't quit" to other adults will boost your child's confidence.
- *Work in a one-on-one partnership with your child.* Whether it's set-

ting a table, making a bed, painting a room, constructing a birdhouse, or working on an important school project, adult-child bonding during projects can make children realize that work is important and that they can be effective workers. Children also love the one-on-one attention they receive while working with partners.

• *Take breaks with your child during projects.* That can include healthy snacks and drinks or talking and laughing. This will help your child recognize the total satisfaction that comes with work.

• *Don't compare your children negatively by telling one that he or she doesn't work as hard as the other.* That will only increase sibling rivalry and cause one child to feel like the worker, while the other feels like the shirker.

• *Be a role model for a positive attitude toward work.* If you take pride in your own work and derive satisfaction from your accomplishments, let your children hear you say, "I did a good job." If you complain about your work, they'll echo your negative attitude about the jobs they're expected to do.

HELPING YOUR CHILD ADJUST TO A NEW SCHOOL ENVIRONMENT

Underachievement patterns frequently begin when children move to a new school. The confidence a child felt in her intelligence at her smaller or easier school can be threatened when she enters a larger and more competitive middle school, high school, or college and encounters many more students who may have better scholastic backgrounds. Although this holds true for all children, overweight children are burdened with disadvantages because they are stereotyped by teachers and peers alike as being dumb and lazy.

As you recall from earlier in this chapter, Terri refused to let stereotypes stop her in middle school as she persevered and worked up to honors classes by high school. Lorie also took advantage of her new college environment to make a fresh start and develop her intelligence. Both Terri's and Lorie's stories show how important fresh starts can be to overweight children, and parents can help their children adjust to new environments by explaining to them how important initial impressions are. Children's overweight bodies may set a first impression, but children can change that by working hard, speaking up, and being actively involved in learning from the get-go. If parents don't prepare their children for entrance into a new school environment, overweight children may literally be cheated out of being perceived as intelligent because of the negative stereotypes associated with being overweight.

It's important for a child to realize when he moves from a smaller school to a larger school that he can continue to feel intelligent without having to be the smartest kid in his class. Assure your child of his intelligence and talent by pointing out his individual strengths. Assure him that he doesn't have to measure up to the smartest kids in the school in order to be smart. If your child believes he must get all A's to make you proud, your unrealistic expectations will cause him to become discouraged. Remember that only a small percentage of children receive all-A report cards, although many children are intelligent.

It's important to have high but realistic expectations for your child. Demanding unattainable expectations will cause your child to feel inadequate and as if he can never please you. He may feel intense pressure, give up, and then underachieve anyway.

TAKING AN INTEREST AND SHARING IN YOUR CHILD'S LEARNING

Children whose parents get involved in their learning have a great advantage in school. If parents enrich their children's knowledge by helping them research information in an encyclopedia, at the library, or on the Internet, or if parents travel with their children to museums or historic sites they've studied, children will learn more and feel ahead of their classmates.

Teaching your child information before she learns it in school, like how to tell time, count money, spell difficult words, understand how the planets revolve around the sun, or draw with perspective, will give her an advantage in school. While children have a better understanding of their school material when parents enhance their children's learning, enrichment encourages a child's feelings of intelligence. Consider your own talents and interests, and share that information with your child. It will certainly make her feel special about her own talents. Also, when your child learns skills from you, she will assume you are interested in learning. Your child will see you as a role model and is likely to believe that if you're smart and interested, she must also be a capable, interesting person.

COMMUNICATING WITH YOUR CHILD'S TEACHERS

Children achieve best when their parents are supportive of teachers. Whether or not your overweight child is already achieving well, it's important for you to be in regular communication with his teachers. Because overweight children are especially vulnerable to peer pressure to underachieve in order to feel included by the in crowd, it's especially important for both teachers and parents to be sensitive to their school accomplishments as well as their peer relationships.

Regular communication with your child's teachers will keep you informed of his progress in school as well as alert you to any signs of emotional or behavioral problems, which could stem directly from his coping with his overweight. If a teacher recommends an evaluation by a school psychologist, you should consider that to be an effort to help your child. However, if you are uncomfortable with a school evaluation, you can take your child to a private psychologist.

Don't expect that only your child will be counseled if you seek professional help. You should also be involved in the evaluation and counseling so that you can carry through with the advice that will help you and your child. Just as it's important for you and your child's teachers to work together, it's equally important for you and the psychologist to work together in guiding your overweight child, whether those issues are related mainly to weight or only to learning. If your child is overweight, do recognize the connection between his being overweight and his social-emotional and learning problems. You can't ignore the weight problems and expect to attack social and educational problems successfully when they're so interconnected.

Some parents feel threatened by the idea of seeking psychological help and feel as if they will be blamed for their children's problems. While it is true you may be asked to make some changes in your parenting style, when you see the positive changes in your child, you'll understand the value of the change. If you don't find the psychologist to be helpful, you can always choose not to return or try another psychologist.

How Teachers Can Communicate with Children about Weight

The positive and negative stories about teacher-student relations in the first part of this chapter prove that teachers can be very helpful or very hurtful to overweight children. As a supportive parent, you can facilitate help from teachers and prevent, or at least halt, the hurt prejudiced teachers may cause.

Here are some ways you can encourage teachers to assist your child with a weight problem.

- Identify your child's favorite teacher or coach in academics, sports, dance, music, or art classes.
- Make an appointment to speak with the teacher or coach about your child.
- Explain to the teacher or coach that he or she is your child's favorite teacher, and ask him or her to:

1. Talk to your child privately about her success to build your child's confidence.
2. Express that eating healthy and exercising would undoubtedly make your child even more successful.
3. Suggest someone who could help your child with a health improvement program.
4. Privately acknowledge your child's weight loss if your child is successful.

If a teacher makes a special effort, your child may or may not tell you about it, but be ready to support your child's new efforts. Also, be sure to inform teachers of their impact and thank them for their important contributions.

When Prejudiced Teachers Hurt Your Child's Feelings

If your child is unfortunate enough to have a teacher who is prejudiced about overweight children and your child tells you about an insult or embarrassment caused by the teacher, here are some guidelines.

- Check the facts; ascertain that your child has been honest with you.
- Assure your child that she is a good person and that other teachers have said so as well.
- State to your child that you expect her to continue to work hard and be respectful despite the teacher's prejudiced remarks.
- Tell your child that you plan to report the problem to the principal.
- If your child prefers you don't file a report, explain that you must be fair to other children and that you are almost certain reporting the incident will prevent the teacher from insulting others.
- Report the problem to the principal or appropriate supervisor.
- Point out other good qualities of the teacher to the principal, if possible.

ENCOURAGING HEALTHY NUTRITION, WHICH FOSTERS LEARNING

You should consult your physician for an overall nutritional plan for your children, but I want to include some nutritional tips based on my clinical experience and research, as well as from Dr. Amen. Because overweight children may also be undernourished, may skip meals to hide their overeating, or may feed their emotional sorrows by overloading on simple carbohydrates, these general suggestions may help your overweight children learn better in school.

- *If your child has problems concentrating, check with her physician for the presence of food allergies.* Wheat and dairy products are allergies that may affect children's concentration, although probably only a small percentage of children are affected by them.

• *Insist that your child eat three meals a day as well as one or two healthy snacks.* Skipping breakfast or lunch may adversely affect your child's concentration. Breakfast should include a protein, such as egg, cheese, lean meat, or nuts. Younger children usually require an additional midmorning snack.

• *Avoid making your child breakfast foods that are high in simple carbohydrates.* Foods like doughnuts, muffins, bagels, cinnamon buns, and sugary cereals cause children to feel tired, spacey, confused, and inattentive.

• *Encourage your child to eat breakfasts rich in complex carbohydrates.* Complex carbohydrates from fruits, vegetables, and whole grain products are less likely to provoke inattentiveness.

• *Prepare foods high in protein and iron.* Proteins that include iron are essential for proper body and brain function. The healthiest forms of protein that include iron are chicken, turkey, lean beef, fish (especially tuna and salmon), low-fat cheese, milk, and soy-based products. Fortified cereals also contain iron.

• *Include monounsaturated fatty acids and especially omega-3 fatty acids in family meals.* Foods that include these healthy forms of fat include olive oil, canola oil, and avocados. Omega-3 fatty acids, which are especially important for brain function, are found in cold-water fish (like salmon and tuna) and nuts.

ENSURING THAT YOUR CHILD TAKES THE PATH TO ACHIEVEMENT

Earlier in this chapter I pointed out how similar overweight and underachievement are, and how vulnerable overweight children are to underachievement. For more detailed techniques on reversing underachievement, I suggest you consult my book *Why Bright Kids Get Poor Grades and What You Can Do about It.*

For now, consider how you can help your child take the right path to a healthy weight and healthy school accomplishments. Don't encourage your child to assume he can have a body or an appearance like those he sees on TV, nor can we expect every child to be a Nobel Prize winner. But your child should expect to have a healthy, energetic, active body that he has good control over, as well as an intelligent, hardworking, and productive mind. In order to achieve healthy minds and bodies, children need to work steadily, persevere, overcome barriers, accept adult limits, and develop personal self-control. If they can accomplish these things, then success is theirs, almost regardless of their genetic inheritance.

So while working hard and persevering may not sound exciting to your child, that's what you must encourage and support. Feeling smart and healthy will be the path that leads to the most fulfilling and rewarding life for your child. Even if overweight children concentrate on school in the absence of an exciting social life, it is likely to lead them to eventual success. Of course, you'll want to encourage some time for fun as well, but good achievement in school is the path best taken for personal satisfaction and long-term success.

CHAPTER 5

COUCH POTATOES AND MOUSE POTATOES:
The Less Active Interests of Overweight Children

Physical activity is central to the cause of—and solution to—children's weight problems. Along with diet, it is the most fundamental way to help your child move toward a healthy weight and overcome any genetic disposition he may have toward gaining weight. But just as poor eating habits can both cause weight gain and become a comforting escape for overweight kids, refraining from participation in physical activity contributes both physically and emotionally to their plight.

My survey found that overweight children were less active and athletic, watched more television, and spent more time at their computers than average-weight children. Although these results were not unexpected, the extent of the inactivity of overweight children is staggering and emphasizes the urgency to increase their activity and involvement levels through family and school intervention. Parental involvement will help children improve their physical condition as well help them connect socially and, through achievement, increase their self-confidence and self-esteem.

PART I—THE FINDINGS

My survey found dramatic differences in children's participation in activities related to how they described their weight. The survey found that for every variable related to exercise involvement, overweight children participated less than average-weight children. And compared with average-weight children, overweight children tended to be more involved in passive activities that did not involve physical exercise.

My survey found:

- Overweight children indicate sports interests less frequently than average-weight children. The differences are particularly severe among girls. Instead, overweight children show more interest and participation in arts and music.
- Average-weight children are much more likely to describe themselves as athletic than overweight children.
- Very overweight children spend nearly twice as much time watching television—as much as 3½ to 4 hours per day—as average-weight children.
- Compared with average-weight children, overweight children also spend more time on computers, playing video games, sending e-mail, and using the Internet.
- Overweight children spend considerably more time alone than average-weight children—for very overweight children, approximately 1 hour more daily.

THE IMPORTANCE OF EXTRACURRICULAR ACTIVITIES AND ATHLETICS

Children's involvement in extracurricular activities and athletics is crucial for their future; research has documented that participating in extracurriculars correlates with higher grades in school at elementary and secondary levels. The *See Jane Win* research that I conducted several years ago on the childhood environments of successful women showed that involvement in positive school activities was often related to the women's successful careers. When they participate in interesting activities, children build self-confidence and are more likely to be connected to more positive peer groups. They then become less likely to be involved in high-risk behavior, including alcohol and drug use, violence, and sex.

Further research shows a positive correlation between sports involvement and school grades. Sports require children to discipline themselves by learning to follow rules, respect limits, persevere, deal with success and failure, and push themselves to perform at their best. The same discipline skills translate to what's necessary for school achievement, healthy eating, and healthy lifestyle choices. And that makes sports crucial for overweight children because healthy sports experiences lead to healthy achievement, eating, and life experiences.

ATHLETIC ACTIVITY

In my research, boys tended to perceive themselves as more athletic than girls (see figure 5.1). It's interesting to note that in all weight categories, even the very overweight one, higher percentages of boys than girls considered themselves to be athletic. Despite the implementation of Title IX legislation, which requires schools to equalize sports funding for boys and girls, boys continue to be more involved in athletics than girls.

Still, the very overweight and somewhat overweight boys were less likely to see themselves as athletic than were the average-weight boys. Just under half (48 percent) of the somewhat overweight boys and just over half (53 percent) of the very overweight boys described themselves as athletic, compared with 70 percent of the average-weight boys. For girls the differences were even greater—the average-weight girls were twice as likely to describe themselves as athletic than the very overweight girls (61 percent to 30 percent).

All of the successful adult men interviewed had been active in sports when they were younger. The men's interests seemed to emerge naturally, with the exception of Harry, who fought exercise. He only liked to play indoors, paint, or read. After his mother signed him up for hockey, he gradually became much more physical. Not only did Harry's mom increase his

Figure 5.1
Self-Description of "Athletic,"
by Sex and Weight Category

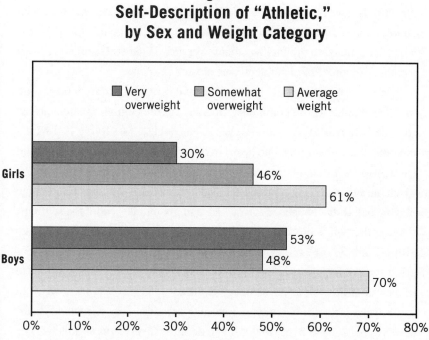

activity level, but she rarely allowed him to watch TV. Harry appreciated his mother's insistence on his playing sports and watching less TV; he went from being the slowest, fattest kid to the fastest kid on the playground.

Your children will eventually appreciate your encouragement toward activities and limits for screen time, too, although they may not thank you now. Even though Harry was overweight for only a short time in his life, much of his present motivation to stay in shape comes from his fear that he might revert to being "the fat kid" he used to be.

Consider the findings on criticism and physical activity by researcher Myles Faith, Ph.D., assistant professor of psychology at the University of Pennsylvania School of Medicine in Philadelphia and his colleagues. According to their study of 576 fifth- through eighth-graders, children whose families or peers criticized their abilities in sports and other physical activities were less likely to be involved in sports and tended to have a negative attitude toward sports and physical activities. The researchers also found that criticism was more commonly directed at girls than boys, and at heavier children more than at lighter children. It's natural to conclude that this criticism contributed to my findings that fewer girls in general, and fewer overweight children of both genders, participated in sports.

Taunts are undoubtedly the worst kind of criticism. Matt, a 6-foot-tall middle schooler whose comments I included at the beginning of chapter 1, shared his hurtful story with me. When he caught a fast flying ball with a moaning "Ow, that hurts," he heard his coach call him a "nanny boy" loud enough so all his teammates could hear. Perhaps the coach was only trying to encourage his acting a bit more macho, but would you want to continue playing ball if that happened to you? Kids in my middle school focus groups told me that when boys see a fat kid running in gym, they say things like "Run, Chubby, run" or "Look at that fat kid go." Teacher, family, or peer criticism will feel devastating to children who may already lack confidence in their coordination or physical appearance.

For the girls in my study, the more overweight they perceived themselves to be, the less likely they were to describe themselves as athletic. The adult women interviewed also confirmed a dislike of sports. Phyllis, for example, hated sports when she was younger. In elementary school, Phyllis was on the soccer team, but she'd daydream and play with leaves instead of focusing on the soccer ball. She also considered her brother to be the athlete in the family. Since he was good at sports, she automatically assumed she was not, and didn't even bother trying. Phyllis's lack of confidence may have been related to her poor coordination or to the lack of praise she received. Her athletic brother probably received plenty of it, while overweight Phyllis no doubt measured her lack of praise in light of the praise her brother received. And this lack of praise may have actually made her feel criticized by comparison to her brother. How often I have heard children in my clinic say things like "My mom (or dad) never thinks I'm as good as my brother (or sister)," even when the parents have never made the comparison.

Doreen, an adult interviewee, at least tried basketball when she was young, but she found her weight didn't leave her the stamina to play. It's reasonable to assume that if Doreen had been praised for her skills by her coach, she might have continued to play sports. Unfortunately, it's also reasonable to assume that it might have been difficult for coaches to praise her skills if she was poorly coordinated, overweight, and out of breath. Perhaps Doreen's mother, like Harry's mother, could have insisted that Doreen persevere in order to build her stamina. Her mother might have asked the coach to encourage Doreen, which might have worked, but coaches are rarely excited about encouraging overweight, out-of-breath players who may actually hurt the team. At any rate, you can see the difficulty for an overweight girl and her parents.

Nina, another adult interviewee, did absolutely no exercise, and in our interview exclaimed: "Oh, my God, gym was traumatic for me! I was heavy and uncoordinated, and embarrassed to dress in front of the other kids." Dressing in the locker room was a special challenge. Nina was ashamed of being fat and would use one special dress on her gym days. She was always worried that girls would see how fat she was, but her dress covered her well while she changed in the farthest corner of the locker room. Not only did Nina hide her body in the locker room, she also avoided sports because she never believed she was good at them.

Another case in point is Terri, who believed she was too big to try out for cheerleading and didn't think there were any girls' sports she could try out for. Instead, Terri immersed herself in drama and music. Girls who feel inadequate about their physical condition and embarrassed about their overweight bodies are unlikely to keep experimenting with different sports until they find one they can enjoy.

Very few of the successful adult women interviewed were athletic as girls, but several gave sports a try, and a few even excelled. Susan played T-ball for a few years in elementary school. She could hit the ball, but she couldn't run to catch it. Although Susan liked playing, she felt weird because she was the only chubby girl on the team. She was afraid to be friendly to other kids because she was waiting for someone to make fun of her for being fat. Susan was so accustomed to being taunted about her weight that she concentrated on her anxiety instead of playing the game, and eventually she just gave up. Often, children who are constantly teased assume that others are noticing their awful weight even when no one says anything. They are simply overly self-conscious and can't move their concentration from themselves to the game.

Lorie attempted volleyball, gymnastics, dance, T-ball, and basketball. She never became proficient at anything, though, because she never followed through. Like Susan, Lorie was afraid everyone watching her would think she was fat, and she never felt skilled enough to play. For example, Lorie would be on the verge of tears during and after each volleyball game because she believed she was such a bad player.

Gail was reasonably active during her youth—running, biking, and walking—although she didn't participate in any organized sports. She was even fairly well-coordinated, but she clearly remembered the time she pretended to be sick to avoid going to an ice-skating party. She feared that if she fell on the ice, she would have a difficult time righting her heavy body. Gail's fear of embarrassment was long lasting, and during our interview she recalled how she has avoided taking her own children ice-skating, even though she is no longer overweight. She resolved to change that in the future, and that determination will help Gail and her children to stay active.

Nancy was one of the few women interviewed who were consistently active during childhood. She considered herself a tomboy while growing up. She claimed she couldn't run very well because she lacked stamina. When she went bike riding with her sister and her sister's friends, she couldn't keep up with them and they would leave her behind. She'd go crying to her mom, who wasn't at all sympathetic to Nancy's overweight. The defining moment for Nancy was her failure to make the cheerleading squad. She tried cross-country racing then but couldn't keep up with the other girls. Determined to lose weight, she said to the cross-country coach, "I'm not good. I suck, but I know you meet after school every day and I want to do it. So I'll walk the course until I get better." Eventually Nancy made both the cross-country and cheerleading teams. Today she's an athletic trainer.

Amanda was another exception of the women interviewed. Like Nancy, she considered herself a tomboy. In high school, at 5 feet 6 inches tall and 180 pounds, Amanda was very active in sports and did hard-core running

CHEERLEADING CONVINCED PATTI

Patti played basketball, but she wasn't very good. She described herself as "sluggish" until she made the cheerleading squad in high school. Patti lost 10 pounds while cheering, and that sparked her first recognition that exercise could really help her. Involvement in sports or an exercise activity can help children realize the relationship between their activity level and weight loss and can motivate them to continue exercising.

and tripping drills for 3 hours a day, 6 days a week. She was in great shape but nevertheless was overweight because she consumed huge amounts of soda pop, candy bars, and unhealthy cafeteria food. Her mother smothered the family meals with sour cream or cheese, and Amanda happily cleaned her plate and topped her meals with more treats. Her bad habits became worse by college, where she increased the amount of food she ate but discontinued her strenuous activity. She quickly learned that she needed to do the reverse—increase her physical activity and taper her eating.

In my survey, sports participation was much less for both very overweight boys and girls, and only slightly less for those who were somewhat overweight (see figures 5.2 and 5.3 on pages 116 and 117), compared with average-weight children.

Other research shows very clearly the relationship between overweight and lack of exercise. For example, the 1999 Youth Risk Behavior Survey was a component of the Youth Risk Behavior Surveillance System, which was developed by the Centers for Disease Control and Prevention in Atlanta in collaboration with representatives from 71 state and local departments of education and health, 19 other federal agencies, and national education and health organizations. In that survey, researchers found that boys were involved in both moderate and rigorous physical activity more often than girls and that those youths who were involved in higher levels of physical activity were less likely to be overweight. There's no surprise in the findings

Figure 5.2
Favored School Activities (Boys), by Weight Category

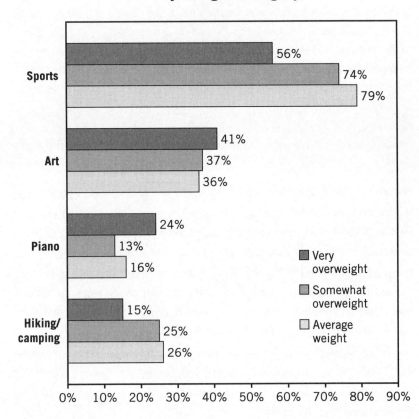

that boys between ages 8 and 16 were less likely to be overweight if they participated in sports or exercise programs. The same held true for girls between the ages of 14 and 16.

In another study of children's activity, more than 50 percent of the children reported themselves to be inactive. The percentage of those who were inactive increased to 63 percent by the time they reached adolescence. The authors hypothesized that lack of exercise may be a more serious cause of obesity than consuming too much high-calorie food.

Figure 5.3
Favored School Activities (Girls),
by Weight Category

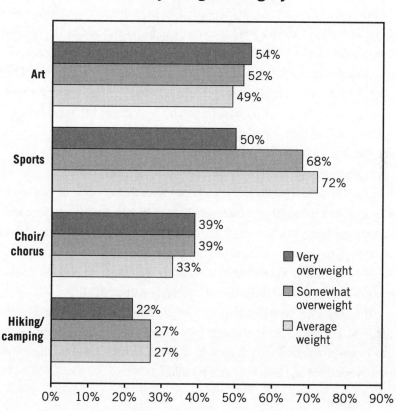

In a study that followed 1,213 African-American girls and 1,166 White girls from ages 9 to 19, Sue Kimm, M.D., and colleagues at the University of Pittsburgh School of Medicine found a dramatic decrease in physical activity for both African-American and White girls by the time they reached adolescence. At ages 16 and 17, 56 percent of the African-American girls and 31 percent of the White girls reported no physical activity during their leisure time. Girls who had been more overweight to begin with showed an even greater decline in physical activity.

In their National Association for Sport and Physical Education (NASPE) report, researchers Charles Corbin, Ph.D., professor in the department of exercise and wellness at Arizona State University and coauthor of *Fitness for Life*, and Robert Pangrazi, Ph.D., professor in the department of kinesiology at Arizona State University in Mesa and author of *Dynamic Physical Education for Elementary School Children*, pointed out that "calories expended in childhood and youth can help control body fatness." They maintained that children who expend calories when they are young are more likely to do so later in life. The researchers concluded that achieving a higher caloric output is perhaps the best remedy for the higher caloric intake that is a characteristic of modern society.

Sadly, only one-third of schools now offer physical education classes, and many of those that do provide classes have them only 3 days a week. Schools blame financial constraints. In light of the fact that overweight children are less likely to choose extracurricular sports, active daily gym classes are an even more important priority for them. You may notice I mentioned *active* gym classes. That's because all of us remember some gym classes where we stood around more than we actively participated.

The only other physical activities listed on my survey were hiking and camping. These activities also had significantly less participation by the very overweight children, but no significant difference between the somewhat overweight and average-weight children.

THE ARTS ARE IMPORTANT
FOR OVERWEIGHT CHILDREN

Music and art participation is an excellent idea for all children, regardless of weight. Music and art are wonderful enrichment and social activities, and involvement in these activities also seems to be related to achieving higher grades. Unfortunately, they do not provide much-needed exercise, so as parents we want to encourage our children to explore these strengths and interests but also to find time for physical activities.

According to my research, overweight children were somewhat more involved in these nonphysical activities (see figures 5.2 and 5.3 on pages 116 and 117). As I mentioned earlier, it is likely that their more frequent involvement in these activities is related to their lack of participation in sports. Sports involvement often requires so much practice that it allows less time for involvement in other activities.

In my adult interviews, more women than expected had been interested in art, music, or drama. These were healthy outlets for all of the women but may have precluded opportunities for physical fitness. Gail played the oboe and majored in music. Susan's father was impatient with her and would give her a coloring book and tell her to sit down, be quiet, and draw, so Susan learned to love art. Sally was always interested in art but confessed to using her artwork as a hideaway. Instead of going to eat in the cafeteria, she'd get a pass and go to the art room instead. She had a talent for creating things and doing crafts, and more than compensated for her missed lunch by scarfing down food when she arrived home to an empty house with an empty stomach.

SCREEN TIME
AND THE OVERWEIGHT CHILD

The direct relationship between screen time and weight groups emphasizes an extreme problem for overweight children. The overweight boys in my research, even more than girls, spent many more hours in front of a television or computer screen than average-weight boys (see figures 5.4 and 5.5 on pages 121 and 122). (There may be some overlapping in these reported hours, specifically with children's playing games or writing e-mail, because children were given the opportunity to check the number of hours for each.) In any case, television, video games, e-mail, and the Internet seem to fill the days of overweight children. It's very clear that these couch potatoes and "mouse potatoes" are not burning off calories.

My adult interviewees grew up before computers were able to add to their inactivity, but notice what some of the women had to say about their television time.

TV Dinners

I ate in front of the TV, since our kitchen table had only two chairs. When we'd eat, we'd take our plates and go into the living room and watch TV. I had a TV in my room and always watched a lot before bed.

Sally, adult interviewee

No Active Interests

My favorite activities were going to the movies and dragging Main with my friends and stopping to talk to other kids. I had no interest in sports or extracurricular activities.

Doreen, adult interviewee

Her World Was TV

If I filled out an application that asked for my hobbies, I'd think, *This is ridiculous. I have no hobbies.* All I did was watch TV. I didn't have any hobbies because I thought I'd have to be perfect at something to enjoy it.

Lori, adult interviewee

Susan Looks beyond the Television

Our world revolved around TV. We never did anything else, no game playing or reading. Everything was TV. Now that I'm thinner and healthier, my world doesn't revolve around food and TV. I've discovered many new interests. My time spent thinking about food and eating converted to time for exploring a formerly undiscovered, and interesting, world.

Susan, adult interviewee

Researchers have suggested that obesity risks could be cut by approximately one-third if the average television-watching time decreased from

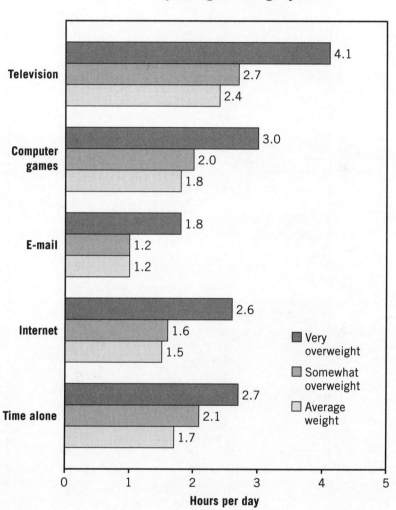

Figure 5.4
**Screen Time and Alone Time (Boys),
by Weight Category**

3 hours a day to 1 hour a day, but findings have indicated that overweight children watch more television than that. A study of 2,971 youths between ages 8 and 16 found that girls who watched 4 or more hours of television a day were more likely to be overweight than those who watched less than 4 hours. Another study of youths between ages 14 and 18 found a pronounced

Figure 5.5
Screen Time and Alone Time (Girls),
by Weight Category

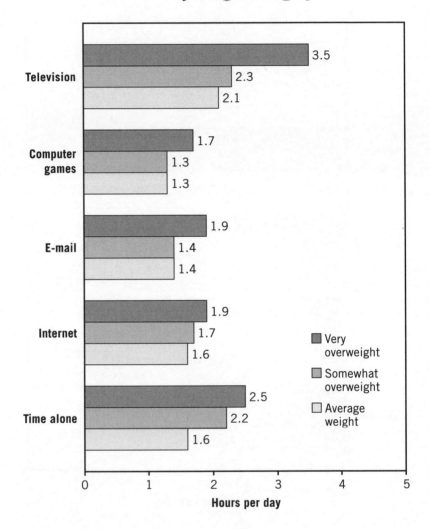

relationship between TV watching and overweight. In a study based on more than 15,000 high school students, Joey C. Eisenmann, Ph.D., who works in the department of health and human performance at Iowa State University in Ames, and colleagues compared teens who watched less than

1 hour of TV a day with those who watched 2 to 3 hours, and 4 or more hours. The researchers found that the more TV teens watched, the more likely they were to be overweight. Incredibly, approximately 25 percent of the high school students watched 4 or more hours of TV a day.

In addition to not burning any calories watching TV, children are often munching away as well. Leonard Epstein, Ph.D., professor of pediatrics at the University of Buffalo in New York, maintains that the average child eats 600 calories a day in front of a TV.

Harry was the only adult interviewee who mentioned that his parents limited how much television he watched. Among the middle school children in my focus groups, there was considerable variation for their parents' limits on screen time. Some children talked about definite limits that they respected, other children said their parents didn't mind what they watched, and a third group acknowledged that their parents set limits, which the children then ignored or defied frequently.

Matt, who you will recall did not really like football or sports in general, responded with enthusiasm when I asked him about this interest in computers and television. His mother thought he'd probably never leave the computer screen if she didn't limit his screen time.

As early as the preschool years, television watching has been shown to be related to children's being overweight. A study of 2,700 preschool children in lower socioeconomic groups concluded not only that television watching was an early serious threat to children's weight but also that having a television set in children's bedrooms increased the likelihood that these very young children were overweight. Approximately 40 percent of the preschool children studied had television sets in their bedrooms. I wish I could convince all parents to never put a television set in children's bedrooms.

Not only are overweight children watching more television than average-weight children, but they are also watching more commercials for unhealthy eating. A study reported at the Asia Pacific Scientific Forum of the American Heart Association showed that Saturday-morning children's commercials have shifted from an emphasis in 1976 on sugary breakfast cereals to the "fun" atmosphere of fast-food restaurants in 1992, and, in 2001, to the value of larger "kid-size" portions available at fast-food restaurants. No wonder overweight children grow even fatter. Watching these commercials may cause them to feel hungrier and lure them to the kitchen for unhealthy snacks. They then return to the television set to polish off their snacks.

Even scarier is a report given by Caroline Oates, Ph.D., and researchers of the University of Sheffield in England at a recent meeting of the British Psychological Society. Through interviews with 182 children, they found that children between ages 4 and 9 assume that advertising material is information and don't recognize its sales or persuasive content. It wasn't until age 10 that children realized that TV ads were intended to persuade them to buy products. These young children may feel that they're following adult instructions appropriately when they eat the unwholesome foods advertised.

HOME ALONE

With more parents working than ever before, children are spending more time at home alone. Figures 5.4 and 5.5 on pages 121 and 122 showed that very overweight boys and girls spent an average of 2.7 hours and 2.5 hours alone a day, compared with somewhat overweight boys and girls at 2.1 and 2.2 hours and with average-weight children at 1.7 and 1.6 hours.

Spending so much time alone may cause other problems. Deborah Vandell, Ph.D., works with the Wisconsin Center for Education Research at the University of Wisconsin, Madison. In a 2003 study, she and her colleagues studied the after-school habits of 191 eighth-graders. The researchers found that the children who were enrolled in after-school programs were more likely to be found doing homework, enrichment activities, sports, or volunteer services and less likely to be eating or watching TV than those not enrolled (see "Student Activities at After-School Programs and Elsewhere").

The significant connection between children who were eating more frequently and were not in school programs reinforces the connection between loneliness and overeating. Also, the study indicates the importance of eating as a habit because those enrolled in programs were typically unaccustomed

STUDENT ACTIVITIES AT AFTER-SCHOOL PROGRAMS AND ELSEWHERE

	HOURS PER DAY	
Activity	No program	At program
Homework	6.3	10.6
Enrichment	5.7	19.2
Eating	11.0	2.6
TV	19.5	0.6
Sports	5.4	32.4
Volunteer service	0.1	3.5

Reprinted with permission from the presentation "When and Why After-School Programs Support Children's Development," Deborah Lowell Vandell, University of Virginia, 3/14/03.

to eating during programming and were then less likely to eat at home on days when they were not in programming. Moving children from inactivity to healthy activity seems an important goal of the rescue techniques, and after-school care seems a healthier alternative to regularly leaving children at home alone.

PART II—RESCUING TECHNIQUES

Children are born with different temperaments and varying activity levels, and it may be true that part of the reason that some children are overweight is that they have genetically low activity levels. However, unlike much of the nutritional research that often seems contradictory and inconclusive, research on the need for exercise is completely consistent: Exercise is good for your health and excellent for your children's health as well. The National

Institutes of Health recommends at least an hour a day for adults and even
more for children. Parents should take this recommendation seriously for
themselves and for their children. This section will guide you to:

- Use praise to encourage your children's participation in athletics
- Encourage play for family bonding and activity
- Select sports for your children
- Support your children in developing new interests
- Balance children's screen time with physical exercise
- Monitor children's time alone
- Foster physical activities in schools

THERE'S THAT PRAISE AGAIN

In case you think this is merely repetition, note that it is *vital* repetition. If
the praise given to children reflects parents' values and expectations, overweight children are unlikely to believe that physical activity and exercise
are important for them unless they are praised for some athletic skill. Although a minority of our adult interviewees had extremely good coordination—all the men played sports as kids, both Patti and Nancy made the
cheerleading teams, and Amanda was a basketball star—most of the women
avoided athletics like the plague. Even when they were capable, the women
typically assumed their audience would be scrutinizing their fat bodies instead of watching the game. It obviously is much more difficult to praise
athletic skill when children are so self-conscious that they won't play at all.

Praise for physical activity should start very early, when young children
are still oblivious to how awkward or fat they appear compared with other
children. If you voice your delight at your child's performance, he'll keep
dancing, but if you're disappointed at his lack of gracefulness, he'll drop
out. Children rarely compare their own grace with that of other children;
they only compare the compliments they receive. Some parents are so worried about the performance of their overweight children that they won't en-

roll the children in classes at all. Sadly, such parents continue to refer to their children as klutzy, clumsy, and awkward because they're overweight. It took some courage on my part to foster athletics for our daughter, Sara, but I'm glad I did (see "Sara, Please Forgive Me!" on page 128).

Physical activities, sports, gymnastics, dance, swimming, and fitness should be introduced early to all children, but especially to children who have genetic tendencies toward overweight or who are poorly coordinated. If you missed the opportunity to introduce these early, it's never too late. Small dance, gymnastic, or swim classes that don't require performances in front of large audiences can entice middle and high school kids to discover new skills. Even private swim lessons can be negotiated, similar to arrangements for private piano lessons or tutoring. When tweens and teens discover that their activity causes them to lose weight, as it did for Patti the cheerleader, they're more likely to get into the exercise habit. Like tutoring, small group or private classes may actually help your adolescent to catch up on a skill and develop enough confidence to join a large group class.

Moderate, noncompetitive praise works best. Phrases like "Hey, you're pretty good," "You've got rhythm," "You're really learning," "You hit that ball hard," "Terrific flexibility," "You're running faster," and "What fun you're having" are general but honest and encouraging compliments to keep your children active. If you can't in good conscience praise your child's performance, perhaps you can at least comment positively on her improvement and effort. You don't need to tell her she's "the best" dancer, gymnast, or soccer player to keep her active, only that "you're getting better." You may recall from earlier chapters that if you overpraise your child and she can't attain the competitive goals you set, she is likely to feel pressured and drop out. Children don't have to be the best at sports, but they should learn to *try* their best.

And when your child's team does their best—or wins!—it's okay for your child to celebrate with the team's ice cream treats after successful recitals or games. Occasional celebration with food as others do will help to prevent your child from feeling deprived and will also help to maintain and increase her activities.

SARA, PLEASE FORGIVE ME!
YOUR STORY WILL HELP OTHER MOTHERS

My youngest daughter, Sara, followed in birth order a sister who was a cheerleader and a dancer, and two very athletic brothers. Initially, Sara did not have the same natural grace as her siblings. Other parents would probably have called her awkward. She didn't even start to walk until she was 21 months old, surely setting some kind of record for slow walking among toddlers. Nevertheless, by age 3 and thereafter, Sara danced, pliéd, tapped, tumbled, skipped, swam, and sank for many years.

From early on, I applauded her recitals and her practices. Although only her awkwardness was outstanding at times, Sara hardly realized she was unusual. Even when she had to repeat the advanced beginners swim test eight times between ages 7 and 10, and tears came to my eyes each time she failed, no one ever convinced her that she was unsuccessful. As a result, while she might have never felt like a stunning winner, neither was she allowed to feel like a loser. After she finally accomplished the breathing and stroke coordination, she passed every other level, including lifeguard certification, by the time she was 12.

As a young adult, Sara now swims, windsurfs, inline-skates, ice-skates, does fitness training, and is a wonderful dancer. There is nothing awkward about Sara, and she leads an active lifestyle that is exemplary. Your Sara can, too.

THE FAMILY THAT PLAYS TOGETHER STAYS TOGETHER

From board and card games to backyard baseball and hula hoops, the family that plays together cements a bond that preserves family relationships. Actively playing together rather than merely observing a screen or only passing one another on the way to work or meetings establishes an empowering family relationship. Parents can coach sports and activities so that children are able to learn many new skills. As children mature and teach parents some of their own games, or at least try to outmaneuver their parents in family activities, parents and children have a more level playing field.

Families also communicate more when they play. They talk through the rules of the games they play and the contests they organize in the same way that they solve problems about the rules for living life itself. They learn about good sportsmanship and competition, being kind to younger siblings, collaborating as a team, and most of all taking active control of their lives. From their involvement in family games, they learn to think, plan, strategize, laugh at their mistakes, apologize, run, catch, bike, skate, balance, and persevere.

Families will have to be cautious about being too competitive, particularly if only one child in the family is overweight and other children are better coordinated. Teaming up families so that the better coordinated parent allies with the poorly coordinated child may make for a more balanced team and less discomfort for the child with poor coordination. For overweight children, taking active control of their lives is the key to their health, and family game playing can be instrumental in that lesson.

For parents who aren't accustomed to activity, your involvement is long overdue, but it's never too late to start. If you haven't thrown a football or basketball since middle school, don't know how to keep score for tennis or bowling, or hate sports in general, try jogging, skating, walking, or biking. Order pedometers or speedometers to count your miles and chart your distance. Simulate a walk to California or Florida, or only to a nearby city or park, by plotting your weekly distance on a map. Establish a family reward system for each person who arrives at a destination, whether he gets there first or last. You can double the credited miles for younger children just as the airlines do for frequent flyers. When weather is a factor, visit a nearby gym or a local Y with the family. Perhaps some family friends can join you to make the excursion into a party. Exercising with others for companionship and support will prevent you from backing out at the last minute.

Another option is purchasing a treadmill or stationary bike for your home and considering it mandatory exercise while watching TV. Your children will automatically learn how important activity is to their well-being and their weight control.

The concept that *play is exercise and exercise is play* will reinforce and teach children to make exercise a healthy lifelong habit.

SPORTS FOR ALL CHILDREN

For children who hit the home runs, score winning baskets, are star ballerinas or gymnasts, or even only catch a fly ball in the outfield, motivation comes easily. Winning encourages children to play more, and children who have excellent coordination and opportunities to play sports require no prodding because sports are fun for them. Many overweight children are deprived of winning experiences because they have poor coordination or because their parents assume that their weight precludes their success. Often, parents hesitate to even enroll their children in activities that could cause their children to feel like failures. Parents fear that these activities will further damage their children's self-esteem.

It's best for parents to assume that there are sports for all children, and that with reasonable practice and opportunity, all children can have winning experiences even if they're only part of a winning team.

The Rimm children were told early on that no matter how good they were at an activity, there would always be some children who were better and, fortunately for them, some who were worse. As long as there are children who are worse, it's possible for all children to win, if only occasionally. Fortunately, children who are worse at one activity may be better at another. Parents need to search for opportunities for developing their children's athletic confidence.

The popular team sports—such as baseball, soccer, hockey, and basketball—may or may not work for your overweight child. But she may be very well suited to individual pursuits—like swimming, track, tennis, skiing, golf, or karate—that have the advantage of being lifelong sports she can enjoy all through adulthood. And while cheerleading, gymnastics, tumbling, and dance may be gender-stereotyped for girls, they're great for both boys and girls since all teach competition and self-discipline. Camping, hiking, biking, and canoeing don't have teams, but they require teamwork, provide plenty of exercise, and bring families and friends together. These are particularly good fits for teenagers who might find it's too late to join a competitive team sport filled with highly skilled peers.

Your children aren't required to love sports in order to participate in them. However, they should be expected to participate. You may be surprised to find that once they've given a sport a fair chance and, with some experimentation, found their favorite among them, they'll be excited to participate. If they stamp their feet and refuse to join, you may not be able to force them. You may have to settle for convincing them to ride their bikes, climb some trees, or only walk the dog several times a day. At least that will get them actively out and about. But make no mistake about it; walking the dog around the block is not enough exercise, only a start. Don't give up on convincing them to find more vigorous physical pursuits.

SUPPORTING NEW INTERESTS

In your efforts to motivate your overweight child to participate in sports, don't deprive him or punish his other interests, even if they don't involve physical activity. Overweight children who are interested in debate, drama, music, art, foreign languages, chess, or writing have much better opportunities for developing themselves as fulfilled young people. If you insist that your child must always do exercise-based activities, he'll feel cheated out of his strengths and interests. It's healthier for adolescents to be a little too busy than to devote all their time to hanging around and watching the screens. Participating in music, drama, or art is still more active than watching television or playing computer games.

BALANCING SCREEN TIME

For many reasons beyond weight control, television sets and computers should be located in rooms with full family access. This has become even more critical since the Internet became readily available and accessible. It's important for parents to know what children are watching without children's feeling as if their parents are snooping. Furthermore, television viewing should be a family activity. Children shouldn't watch TV in their bedrooms in order to fall asleep or to entertain themselves when they're not sleeping. Children who get into the habit of watching television during the night become "night people" and don't function very well at school during the day. Television and the Internet can be hypnotic and addicting, and while children can learn a lot and even enjoy many good shows, they won't burn calories when they're hypnotized by the screen.

Some helpful guidelines for your children to follow during their screen time are:

- Don't watch television during family meals.
- While watching TV or using the computer, eat only modest servings of fruits, vegetables, or low-fat protein snacks, and drink only water.
- Exercise at least half an hour for every hour of television or computer time.
- Limit TV time and computer use to 2 hours daily.

If you follow those simple guidelines, you can make occasional exceptions when world events, sports specials, or a particular film or dramatic production invites a little extra screen time. Imagine how you'll need to stock up on fruits and vegetables with those rules! I wish I could give every family a television that would be powered only by the pedals of a stationary bicycle or a moving treadmill. That would surely be effective in either cutting down on television viewing or increasing exercise. Most likely it would accomplish both.

WHAT ARE CHILDREN DOING ALONE?

Latchkey kids are common in America today. Many children arrive home from school and are alone until their parents return from work. For some trustworthy children, spending an hour or two on their own and completing homework or playing with siblings can be trouble-free and even help them establish some independence. However, from my study it does appear that overweight children spend too much time alone, are often lonely, and are probably eating and watching TV to keep themselves company. The Vandell study mentioned earlier about after-school care confirmed that scenario and certainly corroborated my survey findings.

Consider whether your children should be in after-school programs or with a neighbor instead of at home alone. Most after-school programs have an incredible number of work and play activities taking place on the playground; you often hear that humming sound of happy involvement. Even if children are indoors, they'll be doing homework or working on crafts, talking, and busy doing things together.

If your children come home alone, be sure to fill the refrigerator with fruits and vegetables, instead of providing a supply of junk food for snacks. If you take the next step and cut up fruits and veggies and put them out on a plate or in a bowl on the table, they'll look so tempting and accessible that children will help themselves. Plus, a low-fat dip will go a long way in making veggies more palatable and interesting. If only healthy snacks can accompany screen time, you'll soon find your children eating vegetables, instead of Oreos and potato chips. Perhaps the Oreos or chips could be a once-a-week treat, although not while watching TV.

If your children are to be home alone for some time, leave a list of chores and activities that should be completed before you arrive home. Reward your children with special family time if they accomplish their chores. Let them know you appreciate their efforts and that their accomplishments afford you the extra family time together.

PARENTS CAN ACTIVATE SCHOOLS

Schools feel a great deal of pressure to accomplish almost everything for children, from the basic skills to enrichment, special education, and counseling. Some activities are dropped from school schedules and from the budget because of overload and financial restrictions. Physical education has been eliminated or decreased in many schools without complaints from teens or their parents. Teens may not consider gym cool, and their parents are worried about school taxes. In light of how healthy it is for teens to stay active, if your school has cut physical education classes, this is a good time to go to a school board meeting to make your voice heard. Because there is considerable data included in this book about the increasing obesity of children, your factual presentation could help your cause.

I served on a board of education for 12 years, but it was rare for us to have observers or participants. Occasionally, when a parent would call the board of education office to request that a topic be placed on a meeting agenda, we board members would take notice and be anxious to hear the parent's concern. You may never have attended a board of education meeting before, but you can be powerful in bringing about healthy change to your school. Your voice will be heard even better if others join with you. Prepare handouts, and take the time to review why you believe physical activity is critical to the health of children in your school district. You can remind the board members that:

1. The percentage of obese children has more than tripled in the past 30 years.
2. The National Institutes of Health recommends at least 1 hour of exercise a day for adults, and more for children.
3. Active, healthy children will be better learners in school.

You can find further information for your cause at Web sites listed in the appendix. You may be pleasantly surprised to find that schools will listen when parents make themselves heard. Children will learn more if they are healthier, and there is no dispute anywhere about the importance of exercise for good health.

CHAPTER 6

WHAT'S GOING ON WITH MY BODY?:
Coping with Worries Related to Development

All children struggle to some extent as they mature from childhood to adulthood, the transition period called adolescence. The early adolescent years, from about ages 9 to 12, are often referred to as the tween years—beyond childhood, but not yet teenagers. Changing bodies, emotions, friendships, and family relationships coincide to push and pull, causing young people to advance toward adulthood, then regress to childishness, and then inch forward, again and again throughout adolescence. Parents struggle in the stretch and strain of uncertainty as they're never entirely certain of how much freedom, power, and responsibility to grant their tweens and teens. Young people also struggle to determine how quickly they should grasp adult powers and privileges. Some advance and then temporarily withdraw in fear, while others press every limit to its extreme. But these normal and natural twists and turns of adolescence are even more difficult for overweight children.

In this chapter, I'd like to sensitize you to the differences that take place during development for children who are overweight. If your overweight child is likely to deal with adolescent concerns earlier or later than other adolescents, your being alert to her expected differences and knowing how you can help your child cope with them will surely make her adolescent voyage somewhat smoother.

PART I—THE FINDINGS

The conundrums characteristic of adolescence are magnified when children are overweight. In regard to development, my survey showed:

- As children mature, more are likely to perceive themselves as overweight.
- Very overweight children feel pressure to think about sex earlier than average-weight children.
- Very overweight children feel pressure to have nice clothes earlier than average-weight children.
- Worries about not being social enough, not being pretty enough, and being lonely are worse at all grade levels for overweight children, compared with average-weight children.
- Worries about being bullied decrease for all children as they get older, but decrease much less for very overweight children.
- Perceptions of poor self-confidence increase by grade level for all children, but by seventh and eighth grades, somewhat overweight children are twice as likely, and very overweight children are more than four times as likely, to have poor self-confidence as are average-weight children.

WHEN CHILDREN BEGIN TO NOTICE WEIGHT PROBLEMS

Children's perceptions of their physical and sexual development influence when they begin to notice that they have weight problems. As children mature into adolescence, more begin to realize they are overweight. And some children actually become overweight for the first time during adolescent sexual development as biological changes turn normal-weight children to overweight adolescents.

Of course, all adolescents have growth spurts and gain weight during adolescence. Adolescent appetites tend to increase dramatically to meet growth and development needs. But with so much peer pressure on tweens to be thin, even normal weight gain can be frightening. Khana, an attractive, slim African-American girl, shared this story during one of my focus groups.

"I'm Not Fat"

We get weighed in our gym class four times a year, and the gym teacher announces our weights and heights out loud so everyone can hear. Well, I put on quite a bit of weight last time. The kids heard my weight and they all kind of groaned, but I really grew a lot and I'm not fat. I wish they wouldn't announce the weight aloud. I felt pretty bad.

Khana, seventh grade

Khana wasn't even overweight. Imagine how those tweens who are truly overweight or obese feel when others hear of their weight gain!

Why Tweens Notice Overweight

There are three main reasons that many tweens notice overweight for the first time during adolescence. First, hormonal changes in tweens' bodies during sexual development cause them to become interested in having boyfriends or girlfriends. As a result, tweens begin to define the characteristics that are sexually appealing in those who interest them. Second, TV and media have a great deal of impact on how tweens define attractiveness. Programming on MTV, movies that show young people falling in love, and fashion magazines that include only very thin models tip young people off to the fact that society considers only very thin youths to be sexually appealing and beautiful. Third, at about age 11 or 12, children enter what the famous developmental psychologist Jean Piaget termed the formal operation stage of cognitive development, higher-level thinking, which begins in middle school and continues through high school to adulthood. Tweens do considerably more abstract thinking and making comparisons about their world during this phase. They are then able to hypothesize that if boys like thin girls, or if girls like slim boys, they may be out of the running for the dating scene if indeed they are not of a desirable weight.

Adolescents are searching for their identities, trying to determine who they are apart from their parents, and learning how they differ from or are the same as their peers. They continuously make comparisons to siblings, peers, and people on television or in books and magazines. That's the reason they talk so much to other adolescents during this period of time. It's also the reason they become so much more observant of physical characteristics. Sharon remembered that when she was 11 years old, she noticed that her tummy stuck out more than her friend Roberta's; jealous, she wished she were as thin as Roberta.

When Tweens and Teens Notice Overweight

My survey data showed that only 14 percent of our sample considered themselves to be overweight in third and fourth grades. That percentage climbed to 19 percent by fifth and sixth grades and increased to 21 percent by seventh and eighth grades (see figure 6.1). The 2001 Youth Risk Behavior Surveillance, a national and more extensive survey of more than 13,000 high school students, found that 28.8 percent of ninth-graders and 29.8 percent of tenth-graders described themselves as overweight. Apparently, the older children got, the more likely they were to see themselves as overweight. That finding in itself would suggest a more difficult adolescence for overweight children, especially in a society with an increasing obesity problem yet a media obsession with thinness.

The same Youth Risk high school study also found that girls were significantly more likely than boys to describe themselves as overweight. In my survey of middle school students, percentages of students who described themselves as overweight were almost identical for girls and boys, with 18 percent of the girls and 20 percent of the boys describing themselves as overweight. However, it's apparent from other research that by the time girls reach high school, their self-images have been altered dramatically to reflect their concerns related to weight. Girls worry about weight much more than boys do during both the middle and the high school years.

One study of dieting behavior among overweight children found that by age 11, 30 percent of both boys and girls who were overweight had made efforts to lose weight. The study of 2,196 students, conducted by Helen

Figure 6.1
Self-Perception of Being Overweight, by Grade Level

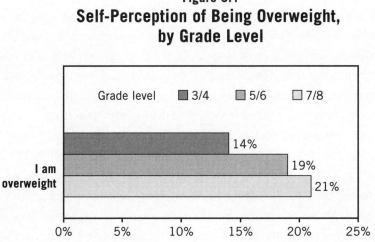

Sweeting, Ph.D., of the University of Glasgow in Scotland and her colleague Patrick West, Ph.D., discovered that those numbers changed by age 15, when only 16 percent of overweight boys, compared with 50 percent of overweight girls, indicated that they'd made efforts to lose weight.

The 2001 Youth Risk Behavior Surveillance discovered a lesser difference between girls and boys, although the findings were in a similar direction. For tenth-graders (approximately age 15), 37 percent of girls, compared with 24 percent of boys, who described themselves as overweight were trying to lose weight. The fact that higher percentages of girls were dieting is indicative of the significant disadvantage girls feel about their appearance for the purpose of attracting boyfriends.

The world is more accepting of large boys, and in some sports, like football and wrestling, an overweight boy can succeed and be admired by his peers because of his size. Size may even give boys some advantages in leadership among their peers by high school. This also explains why there was no significant differential between girls and boys describing themselves as overweight in my middle school study, but there was a great differential for high school students.

My adult interviewees also confirmed my survey finding that as children mature, they are more likely to view themselves as overweight. Very few of the interviewees had considered themselves fat in early elementary school, and those few who did remembered the need to find special-size clothes as their cue to their being different from the normal size of other children. Most interviewees became aware that they were overweight in fifth or sixth grade, when peers taunted them or when their increased interest in the opposite sex alerted them to their weight problems.

The women interviewed had been aware that boys didn't like fat girls, and thus they felt they didn't have the potential to have boyfriends. For the men interviewed, most had made the decision that they enjoyed the social scene and their weight might be a disadvantage in attracting girls. Worries about weight hadn't occurred until late adolescence for the rest, perhaps because boys often mature later than girls. The interviewees said that it was in adolescence that they began comparing themselves with others their age and recognized that being overweight made them different from their peers. Most children don't find it easy to be different during the middle school years, even when the difference is positive. For an overweight child, adolescence is that much more difficult because overweight is almost always considered a negative difference.

THE EFFECTS OF BEING OVERWEIGHT ON EARLY MATURITY

The changing age of sexual maturity for girls has been hypothesized to be related to nutrition and body weight. From 1850 through 1948, the average age of menstruation occurred 3 to 4 months earlier every 10 years, and this trend was most frequently attributed to nutrition. In an extensive study of more than 17,000 girls reported in 1997 in the journal *Pediatrics*, the average age of onset of menstruation—approximately 12.5 years—did not differ significantly from that of girls in 1948. In this study, researchers Marcia E. Herman-Giddens, P.A., M.P.H., Dr.P.H., a senior fellow at the North Carolina Child Advocacy Institute and an adjunct professor in the School of Public Health, Department of Maternal and Child Health at the University of North Carolina in Chapel Hill, and colleagues hypothesized that the lack of changes over the past 50 years may be related to girls' having achieved reasonably healthy nutrition 50 years ago.

While onset of menstruation hasn't changed much in the past 50 years, the study in *Pediatrics* hypothesizes that the start of puberty, characterized by early breast development, may be beginning earlier for girls than formerly believed. The researchers found that 48 percent of the African-American girls and 15 percent of the White girls in the large sample had begun breast development by age 8. This is definitely earlier than what is documented in classic medical textbooks, which makes it tempting to believe that girls are beginning to mature earlier than before. This is important because some experts, like Paul B. Kaplowitz, M.D., a pediatric endocrinologist at the Medical College of Virginia in Richmond, blame early maturity on overweight. Unfortunately, the benchmark research on which the medical textbooks are based is flawed. The standard with which development is being compared was established in the 1960s and was based on 192 girls who lived in an orphanage and may have indeed been undernourished. So we don't really know whether obesity is causing an earlier beginning of puberty for girls or not. But if puberty does begin earlier because more girls are overweight, parents will need to help girls understand the beginning of their sexual development even earlier, as well as the differences in feelings girls may be having, compared with other girls their age who have not begun puberty.

While menstruation clearly marks a beginning of sexual maturation for girls, sexual maturation for boys is much more difficult to assess, and there is much less written about it. Furthermore, there are no hypotheses that physical maturity for boys is occurring earlier now than in previous years, nor that physical maturity for boys is linked to overweight. Boys' maturation takes place at approximately 14 years of age, on average.

The ages when adolescents experience puberty vary considerably from the average, however, and the variations in every middle school class are dramatic, with some girls appearing quite mature by fifth and sixth grades and others not beginning menstruation until age 14. Boys often show even more variation, with some seventh- and eighth-graders looking quite manly, while other juniors and seniors in high school may not yet have begun to grow facial hair.

Social and Emotional Implications

There are social and emotional implications for both early and late maturity, and they are somewhat different for boys than for girls. Because girls, on the average, mature earlier than boys, early-maturing girls and late-maturing boys are at the extremes of any peer cohort group. Late-maturing girls and early-maturing boys tend to be more like the averages or mainstream of middle school classes. For that reason, early-maturing boys and late-maturing girls tend to be more confident and more often chosen as leaders. Early-maturing girls tend not to be as popular and are not as likely to be leaders. Late-maturing boys tend to have the greatest struggle, often behaving quite childishly and lacking confidence as they lag behind all the groups in sexual development.

My survey of middle school children did not include any biological measures of sexual development, but the children were asked to rate their perceptions of their physical development (see figures 6.2 and 6.3 on pages 143 and 144). Sadly again, these findings show another disadvantage for overweight girls and boys.

Compared with average-weight girls, twice the percentage (50 percent compared with 24 percent) of very overweight girls considered themselves to be early developers.

Somewhat overweight girls rated themselves as early developers almost as frequently (42 percent) as the very overweight girls.

The difference between overweight and average-weight boys' perceived early maturity was less than the difference between overweight and average-weight girls'. For boys who considered themselves late developers, very overweight boys (15 percent) ranked at three times the percentage of average-weight boys (5 percent) and were also ranked almost twice as great as somewhat overweight boys (8 percent).

In light of the fact that early maturity for girls is usually a social disadvantage, overweight girls who mature early are likely to have added emotional struggles. They are less similar to the mainstream children and may

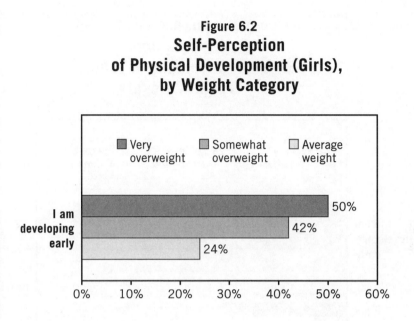

Figure 6.2
Self-Perception
of Physical Development (Girls),
by Weight Category

be interested in having boyfriends when they are as young as 9 or 10. Since boys their age seem quite immature and are not typically interested in girlfriends, these girls are often vulnerable to the attention of older boys. They notice older boys, and older boys notice them and may take advantage of their attentions.

Overweight boys are also farthest from the mainstream in their maturity, often lagging far behind both more mature girls and boys—a fact that, in addition to their weight problems, makes them feel even more different.

THE IMPACT OF EARLY DEVELOPMENT

One of the most obvious effects of earlier maturity was that compared with average-weight children, more of the overweight children worried about sex earlier. As early as third and fourth grades, when only 10 percent of average-weight children felt pressure to think about sex, 15 percent of somewhat overweight and 32 percent of very overweight children worried frequently

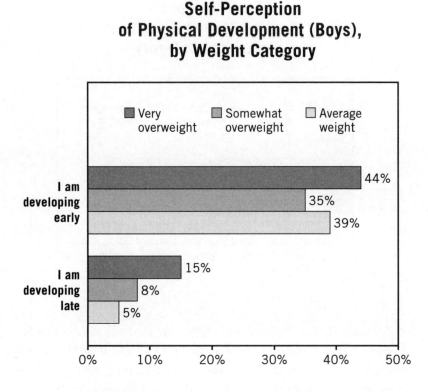

Figure 6.3
**Self-Perception
of Physical Development (Boys),
by Weight Category**

about sex (see figure 6.4). More girls than boys had this concern because
more of the girls were early maturers. Consider that most schools don't introduce health curriculum on menstruation and sexual development until
fifth grade. Furthermore, few parents discuss sex with their daughters before fourth or fifth grade. So these girls may be worrying more about sex
because, except for media sources, they have little access to knowledge of
what sex is all about. They may indeed feel lonely and different in their
early sexual development and unable to talk to friends who are not yet experiencing their bodies' sexual development. Undressing in a swimming or
gym locker room might feel like a nightmare as they worry about other
girls, who haven't yet begun to mature sexually, staring at their developing
breasts and pubic hair.

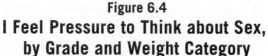

Figure 6.4
I Feel Pressure to Think about Sex, by Grade and Weight Category

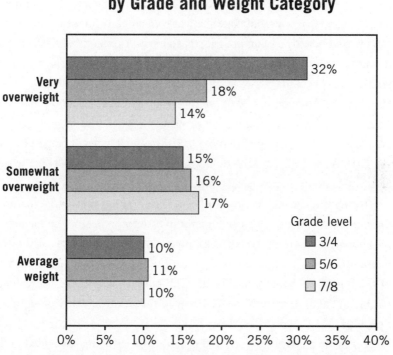

Maturing earlier for girls is accompanied by the mixed feelings of parents of such girls, as well as of the girls themselves. While it is true that girls may feel out of place and self-conscious, sometimes parents can become competitive about their daughters' maturing earlier than others. They may encourage the girls to wear bras before they're necessary, almost as a status symbol for mother and daughter, and brag to their friends about their daughters' changing bodies. And among girls themselves, certainly other girls might envy those who are already wearing bras.

Amanda, an adult interviewee, recalled that very same situation from her childhood. She was the first among her peers to wear a training bra. The taunting was immediate, with innuendos that she was being sexually suggestive. The girls teased her viciously: "We can see your bra through your shirt," "That looks horrible," and "You dress like a tramp." Amanda was in the gifted program at school, and furthermore, she was a tomboy, which added even more differences between her and her peers. She had many friends who were boys, but none she was romantically interested in, yet the girls teased her for having boyfriends so early. The fact that she was maturing faster and was also very smart threatened the other girls, who were jealous that Amanda was "winning" the maturity and intelligence race. However, as Amanda started to gain weight, the girls backed off and were no longer jealous. Gaining weight protected her because she was considered less attractive as a girlfriend to the boys and thus less competition for the girls. As a child, Amanda didn't understand why she was being teased and why it stopped; now as an adult she understands.

Reflecting on her own childhood, Phyllis, another early maturer, thought her overeating was an unconscious defense to stop the meanness of other girls. In effect she could eat away the envy of the girls. She never had a boyfriend in high school because she was always considered "one of the boys." At 5 feet 6 inches tall, 180 pounds, and a size 18, she was strong and active, but felt lonely because she never had any dating relationships.

Lorie, an adult now, wondered if early worries about sex added to the woes of her overweight. Her sexual maturity was at an average age, and she was very interested in having a boyfriend her own age. Yet Lorie harbored fears of sexual molestation by adult men. She hypothesized those fears may have come from her parents' reminders that she "protect herself" from strange men. She also knew a seventh-grade girl who had had a sexual relationship with an uncle. At the time, Lorie didn't realize that the sexual relationship was abusive, nor did her friend, but it fostered Lorie's fear of men. Lorie convinced herself that if she was fat, adult men would not be sexually attracted to her and she would be safe from their leering eyes. She believed that fear might have fueled her to eat even more.

At the time it was a fear she struggled with alone because she didn't discuss it with anyone. If only her mother had spent time listening to Lorie talk about her friends, the story would have emerged. The abuse could then have been reported, and Lorie's friend could have been saved from further abuse. Lorie's mother could also have reassured Lorie of her own safety, or at least encouraged Lorie to talk about her fear of adult men. Perhaps then Lorie wouldn't have felt that she needed to protect her sexual safety, and she would have thus been discouraged from overeating.

The psychological responses of overweight girls may vary among girls. Some may eat to soothe their feelings about not being attractive to boys. Others may eat as a rationalization, believing they can't be attractive to boys anyway so they may as well enjoy their food. They may make the excuse to themselves that "boys just don't like fat girls." Finally, some girls may actually eat more because they are unconsciously afraid to look sexy.

Clothing Woes

Susan was 7 when she began wearing her training bra—no wonder she had difficulty finding appropriate clothes that fit. As in Susan's case, my research showed that worries about having nice clothes were undoubtedly exacerbated for early maturers (see figure 6.5 on page 148). The very overweight and the somewhat overweight children were more concerned about clothing than those of average weight, with four times the percentage of very overweight and twice the percentage of somewhat overweight, compared with average-weight children, concerned as early as third and fourth grades. Perhaps this dramatic early concern came because their early sexual maturity added to their clothes shopping struggles. Children's clothes are not designed for breast development, even if they are chubby sizes. Remember in chapter 3 how Terri's mother helped her shop for a dress, blamed the designers when they couldn't find one, and then sewed an appropriate dress for her? That helped provide Terri with the self-confidence to lose weight when she was ready.

Worries about Social Life

In my research, only a small percentage of children in grades three and four were worried about not being social enough or being lonely, regardless of weight group (see figures 6.6 and 6.7 on pages 149 and 150). By fifth and sixth grades, these worries were substantial for the very overweight and somewhat overweight children. Worries about not being social enough in-

Figure 6.5
I Feel Pressure to Have Nice Clothes,
by Grade and Weight Category

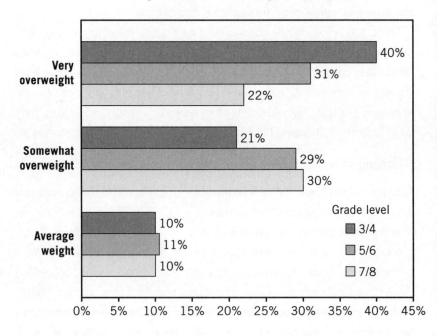

creased for the average-weight children as well, but worries of loneliness stayed about the same. By seventh and eighth grades, more than twice the percentage of overweight children as average-weight children worried about loneliness.

You will recall from chapter 3 that both the negative and positive peer pressure that alerted children to how fat they were tended to manifest itself in fifth and sixth grades, and most of the adult interviewees did describe their middle school years as their most difficult ones. For parents of children this age and teachers of grades five through eight, it's important to realize how perilous this time is for heavy children, and especially for girls.

Lateisha, a slim and very attractive African-American eighth grader, shared her experience (see "Lateisha Is Phat" on page 151). Lateisha's story

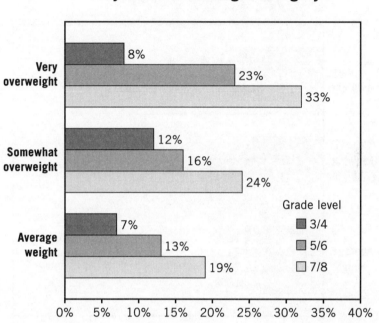

Figure 6.6
I'm Not Social Enough, by Grade and Weight Category

emphasizes how even normal-weight children are worried about the insulting "fat" label. It also demonstrates how swiftly young people can be spurred to desperate, irrational reactions.

Older students were more likely than younger students to indicate that they worried about being pretty (see figure 6.8 on page 152). This, too, was mainly a girls' problem. It held true for all of the girls' weight groups, but the percentages were much higher for those who considered themselves overweight. Several of the interviewees were assured by friends and family that they had pretty faces, which for them meant that in contrast their bodies were not pretty. Paradoxically, this backhanded compliment was found to be reassuring to some and insulting to others. For those who felt reassured, it encouraged them to believe that if they lost weight, they would have an

Figure 6.7
I Worry about Loneliness,
by Grade and Weight Category

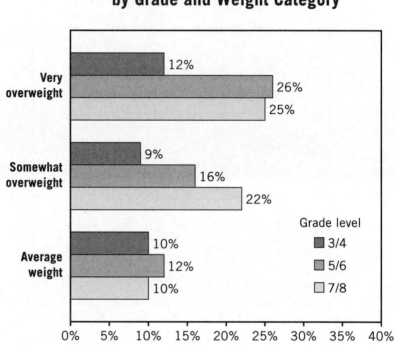

attractive face *and* body. Those who felt insulted by the comment believed that the compliments weren't sincere and that there was no chance that they could lose weight and become attractive anyway.

Although worries about loneliness were shown to be worse for the older children, surprisingly the worries about being bullied declined for all weight groups by grade. However, for those who described themselves as very overweight, the worries about being bullied continued to be very high (25 percent) even in seventh and eighth grades (see figure 6.9 on page 153). Most of the adult interviewees recalled that by around that age they had desperately searched for strategies to stop the insults and isolation, but those were also the grades during which they acknowledged having suffered the worst. Many adolescents do learn to protect themselves from much of the

LATEISHA IS PHAT

I thought I was liked by friends and even considered myself to have a good body, until I overheard a group of guys talking about me. I heard them say I was fat. I was furious and determined to go on a diet immediately. I stopped eating everything but a few carrots and an apple or so a day. I was sad and depressed. I lost weight fast—5 pounds in 5 days. Then I confronted those guys whom I had refused to talk to and said, "Hey, why did you guys call me fat?" They looked confused and then laughed and told me they had called me "phat"—P-H-A-T, not F-A-T—which I guess means being really cool. What a relief! I laughed and went back to eating normally and gained my healthy weight back.

bullying; however, most very overweight adolescents have less confidence in staving off their aggressive peers and continue to suffer. (See "Rescuing Techniques" on page 152 to review some approaches for coping with bullying.)

EARLY DEVELOPMENTAL EFFECTS ON SELF-CONFIDENCE

At all weight levels, the percentage of students with good self-confidence tended to decrease as students got older; that is, the percentage of those who described their self-confidence as poor increased. Sad to say, the higher the children described their weight level to be, the less likely they were to have good self-confidence (see figure 6.10 on page 154). As these children matured and their awareness of being overweight increased, being overweight had an increasingly devastating effect on their levels of confidence. More than twice the percentage of very overweight third- and fourth-graders considered themselves to have poor self-confidence, compared with average-weight third- and fourth-graders. By seventh and eighth grades, that

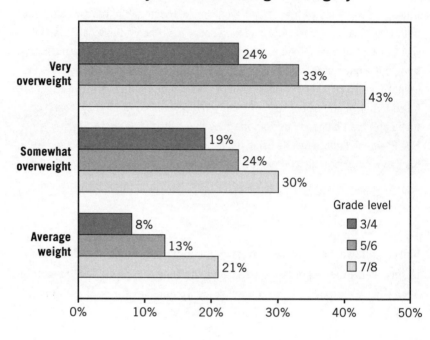

Figure 6.8
**I'm Not Pretty Enough,
by Grade and Weight Category**

percentage worsened so that the proportion of overweight children reporting themselves as having poor self-confidence was more than four times that of average-weight children (see figure 6.11 on page 155).

Family support is crucial during this most difficult time in the lives of overweight children, and sensitive, caring parents and professionals are in the best position to help overweight children develop the self-confidence they most desperately need.

PART II—RESCUING TECHNIQUES

While children are often in a hurry for grown-up privileges and power, 8- and 9-year-old girls rarely feel eager to be the first to develop breasts or

Figure 6.9
I Worry about People Who Bully Me, by Grade and Weight Category

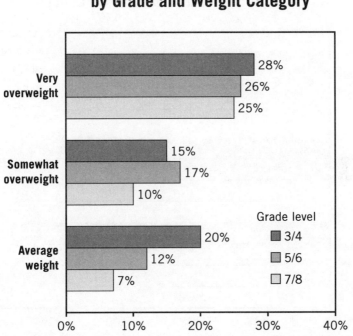

begin menstruation. Nor do seventh- and eighth-grade boys like to be considered babyish by their more masculine or developed peers. Yet more overweight than average-weight children seem to find themselves in both these dilemmas. Rescue techniques to guide parents through the developmental issues of their overweight children include:

- Communicate with children earlier about sex
- Help children cope with jealousy
- Delay dating
- Understand children's sexual fears
- Help children cope with concerns about appearance and conquer the self-confidence struggle

Figure 6.10
I Have Good Self-Confidence, by Grade and Weight Category

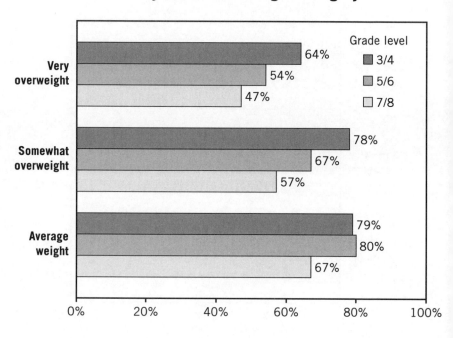

TALKING ABOUT SEX

Children in my middle school focus groups told me that they believed they knew more about sex in second grade than their parents had known in fifth and sixth grades. These children may be exaggerating their knowledge, but today's media surely provided them with a sexual education well before they were able to intellectually or emotionally comprehend the nudity and sexuality on movie screens or the television screens in their own homes. For children whose bodies are also developing earlier than others, watching sex scenes awakens sexual feelings they're unlikely to understand.

While there are usually several years between the first development of breast buds and menstruation for girls, parents should educate them—before the girls begin wearing training bras—about the sexual changes that will af-

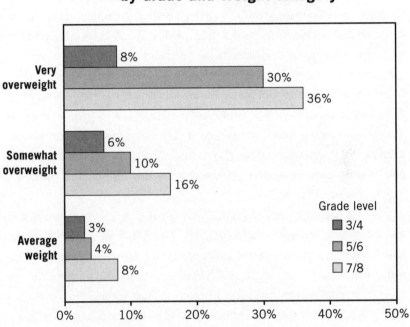

Figure 6.11
**I Have Poor Self-Confidence,
by Grade and Weight Category**

fect their bodies. Considering that other girls their age may not be having similar experiences, a sensitive mother should be an important source of information.

In addition to concerns about menstruation, early-maturing girls need tips about new cleanliness issues. Oily skin and hair as well as underarm perspiration now become concerns that other girls are not yet experiencing. The stereotype of overweight children's being dirty will be more than a stereotype unless parents teach girls about proper hygiene for their maturing bodies. Since your child may still enjoy sloshing around in the mud with her friends, encouraging her to shower more frequently and use deodorant may not fascinate her. Special gift baskets filled with shampoos, deodorants, and shower gels may make her feel privileged, instead of disadvantaged.

I also suggest an excellent book that introduces cleanliness to young girls called *The Care and Keeping of You: The Body Book for Girls* by Valorie Lee Schaefer. It's written at a level that even second- and third-graders would enjoy reading with their parents and in a tempting enough way to invite even a tomboyish girl into the shower. Schaefer's book also explains menstruation and childbirth with illustrations that young girls will understand. The problem with explaining sexual development to your daughter before her friends' parents are even considering it is that you'll have to ask her to keep her new-found knowledge to herself. Since sharing secrets with best friends seems to be part of being an 8- or 9-year-old, unfortunately, not too many little girls are good at keeping secrets from them. If your daughter will have problems keeping this information to herself, you may want to alert the mothers of her best friends, explaining why you are sharing this information with your daughter at an earlier age.

If your daughter matures early, at the age of 8, 9, or 10, and you notice that some of her friends are also early developers, ask the school counselor to hold special sessions for this small group of girls who are ready for information on their changing bodies. These sessions could be supportive for those girls who feel different and prevent them from feeling alone with their early maturity. The standard introductory films on sex always emphasize individual physical differences, which will help the counselor point out that these differences are normal. That in itself should feel somewhat comforting to early-maturing, overweight girls.

Although a fair number of overweight third- and fourth-grade boys in our study also described their development as early, we can reasonably assume that the boys were referring to height and size rather than sexual development. Very few boys begin showing sexual maturity prior to middle school. If your son does seem to be maturing before others, you'll want to discuss sex and his early development with him, but you'll more than likely be able to wait until his school offers classes on the subject. (Schools are usually required to inform parents when these classes take place by having kids obtain permission from their parents to attend.)

For boys who simply grow bigger and taller than most boys, if they are well-coordinated and like sports, they may be good players and thus accepted socially. Being unusually tall and big, however, is not an automatic social advantage. Matt was quick to point out that his size caused people to assume he was 15 or 16, instead of 13 years old. When he lost his temper at the 13-year-old boys in his class who were smaller and looked much younger, he was reminded that he was supposed to control himself. He felt he was expected to act his size, not his age. When I emphasized that he was indeed physically very powerful, he laughingly quoted the closing words from the movie *Spiderman*—"I guess with great power comes great responsibility"—as he crumpled an empty soda can in one hand.

Boys who grow so tall so early need their parents' encouragement to use their strength very carefully. There is real danger that these boys could seriously hurt a small child their age. An adult interviewee who had been tall and big as a child told me that he would use a scowl of disdain to keep kids from taunting him. Small kids were intimidated and disappeared. While that undoubtedly prevented others from teasing him, I doubt that it attracted close friendships. Nevertheless, that was much more effective than the physical fights that eighth-grader Matt found himself in.

You'll recall that my study found that overweight boys tended to mature later than others. Boys who mature late tend to be less interested in peer social life and may feel pressured to worry about both popularity and sex because they don't fit in. Perhaps it's worse for a boy to be teased as a baby, wimp, or fag during that period of time when their peers are far more mature than they are. The "fag," or homosexual, teasing must feel particularly lethal because an immature 13-year-old boy may not have the slightest sexual interest in girls and therefore may start to believe that perhaps he actually is homosexual (see "If Your Overweight Child Is Homosexual" on page 159).

The best predictor of the age at which a boy will mature is the age of maturity of his father. Reassurance by dads or by other males would be particularly helpful to these boys. If Dad or even Grandpa can say, "I wasn't much interested in girls at your age either. I didn't have my first girlfriend until I was 17, but I managed to find your mom (or grandma) eventually. There was nothing wrong with me; I was just a little different," that would be a source of great relief to a boy who hasn't even noticed that girls exist.

THE STING OF JEALOUSY

Although early-maturing girls may not be happy about what's happening to their changing bodies, flat-chested, underdeveloped girls are often envious of early maturers because they worry they may fall behind. Some little girls don't even notice the differences, but more competitive girls may be jealous enough to become viciously mean to early maturers. You'll want to listen to your daughter's concerns and even check with her teachers about their observations in school. If your daughter is hurt by others, it's important to determine whether your daughter is at fault because of poor social skills or she is simply a victim because she's overweight or maturing ahead of the other girls. Once you identify the cause of her problem—and that may not be easy to discern—you'll be able to better explain to your daughter how she can cope.

You will recall that Amanda and Phyllis were early maturers as tweens. If their parents had talked to them earlier about sexual changes, and the girls themselves had felt more confident about their early development, perhaps neither would have eaten to comfort her loneliness. If their parents could have explained that sometimes other kids are mean because they're jealous, Amanda and Phyllis might have been able to respond to peers from a position of either kindness or strength.

A kind approach your daughter might take is "You'll soon be wearing a bra, too. All girls do!" If that doesn't work, your daughter could respond to the teasing from a position of strength. If Amanda or Phyllis had said, "Are you afraid you won't get to wear a bra until you're 14?" it might have stopped the bullies. Amanda and Phyllis didn't have the confidence because they didn't have the knowledge. Parents' advice as to how to respond to bullies may or may not work. But for early-maturing girls, just knowing that a mother or other positive role model understands her unusual situation will go a long way in helping her through it.

We've already talked about bigger and taller overweight boys, but big and tall girls also tend to have great social problems. In my research, both girls and boys considered "being too tall" one of their worries, but it was clearly a much greater worry for overweight girls and boys than it was for

IF YOUR OVERWEIGHT CHILD IS HOMOSEXUAL

If there are indications that your son or daughter is leaning toward homosexuality, you should assure your tween or teen (1) that it's too early to determine whether he is heterosexual or homosexual and (2) that if when he is older it's clear that he is attracted to a same-sex partner, you will continue to love him and accept his homosexuality.

Keep in mind that during adolescence, hormones and sexual attractions are rampant. Tweens and teens may believe they are in love with teachers, coaches, Scout leaders, professional sports stars, or singers on TV. The sexual attraction may feel very powerful and may be very frightening to adolescents, who may keep these crushes secret.

Overweight children who suffer peer rejection and may not be dating when their peers are may assume that such crushes prove they're homosexual. Encouraging them not to rush to conclusions will help. If your child hints of such worries or seem anxious or depressed about her sexuality, arrange for her to see a counselor. Clues to watch for are withdrawing from friends or idolizing adults or stars of the same sex. Children may constantly listen to music by a star, tape pictures of a particular person all over their rooms, or write many letters or e-mails to a star. Any of those actions are normal if teenagers are still involved in normal peer activities. However, if they are also withdrawing from activities, then you should see these as symptoms of more serious problems. Either way, let your adolescent know that you can arrange for her to see a psychologist or counselor if she would like to share any concerns with someone outside the family.

average-weight children. When tall girls become interested in boyfriends, they find very few boys near their size who are interested in girls. They need parents to explain that many of the short boys will be tall eventually and that for most boys maturity is slower than for most girls. You may certainly let your daughter know it's all right to have a boyfriend much shorter than she is, but you'll also want to remind her that there is no hurry to find a boyfriend.

Boys are rarely jealous of other boys based on early maturation alone. Instead, they will tend to be jealous typically if a certain boy is very successful at sports or is in a gifted program. Labeling someone a brain or nerd is a two-way sword; children who wish they were smarter will use social put-downs to disguise their jealousy. Sports envy is less likely to be accompanied by negative comments from peers because sports heroes have such enormous status and power. Thus, jealous boys may express their annoyance subtly by intimating that jocks aren't that smart, but they are usually less effective at causing jocks to lose confidence in the midst of their prestigious success.

WAITING TO DATE

Ten-year-old girls who look 15 are vulnerable to the attentions and flirtations of older boys. Furthermore, overweight girls are often starved for the attention of boys, especially since boys their age are rarely interested in girlfriends. Even if they are, boys are rather cruel to and often reject overweight girls, as the interviews I conducted in my focus groups have shown. Girls this age can find shelter in the development of interests and in involvement in activities like all-girl sports, Girl Scouts, and Girls Inc. Sexual energy can be diverted to extracurricular involvement, which is safer and builds self-confidence.

Additionally, it's fair for parents to delay girls from dating when they're too young to make good decisions. If you allow your daughter to attend girl-boy parties, your daughter should at least be with tweens or teens her age, rather than older kids. You can expect to hear your daughter angrily assert, "Mom, you don't trust me!" You can assure her that you do trust her, but nevertheless at the moment she's too young for dating. She'll undoubtedly give you desperate reasons for her request, but you're best off diverting the conversations to all the activities she can become involved in instead of continuing a no-win argument about dating. You can also assure her that eventually, by high school, you'll allow her to date.

I don't recommend that parents set a particular age for first dates because you may want to allow your daughter to date when a responsible boy her age is interested. She will be heartbroken if she has to turn down an appropriate candidate. And there's nothing magical about a particular birthday for the beginning of dating. If you're too rigid, you'll find that your child will date without your knowledge. Too many young teens have shared with me stories of dates their parents knew nothing about.

THE SEXUAL FEARS OF CHILDREN

Being afraid of "big, bad men" is not new to this generation, nor is it a specific fear for overweight girls; rather, this is a fear for all children. Extensive media coverage of kidnappings and sexual assaults may make children feel that such abductions happen more frequently than they actually do. Furthermore, visual impressions from television may be difficult to eradicate and may exacerbate fears for children and especially for girls, who seem to be victimized more frequently.

Lorie's story of how she had unconscious reasons for eating—that is, to protect herself from looking too sexual—may be one of the more urgent issues for overweight children, although it's unlikely Lorie could have understood that at her age. Plus, fears about older men will be a particular concern of overweight girls who physically mature earlier because they are more vulnerable to the attentions of older men and because, for a small percentage of overweight girls, eating provides protection from believing they are sexually attractive.

Parents should be perceptive of their children's fears. If you notice that your child struggles to fall asleep at night, has nightmares, seems to avoid certain neighborhoods, runs home breathlessly out of fear, or is afraid of going to other children's homes, ask him to share his fears with you. You might even talk to him about some of your own childhood fears, especially those that were needless and imagined, so he won't feel alone. Children should know about "stranger dangers" and be aware that there are risky places that should be avoided, but they also need the security of knowing that most places are relatively safe. Parents have to assess the risks of places that children, and especially daughters, want to visit alone or with friends. Certainly, children should be cautioned to stay away from those areas or homes their parents deem unsafe, but it's important not to be overprotective, or children will either worry unnecessarily or disobey their parents' requests.

APPEARANCE AND
THE SELF-CONFIDENCE STRUGGLE

The techniques for helping children cope with their worries about appearance, clothes, social, and self-esteem issues are the same as those described in chapter 3. This chapter on development establishes that your early-maturing daughter will require your understanding and support sooner than you would normally have expected her to be concerned about such issues, and perhaps sooner than you had such concerns in childhood. A book that I've written for tween girls, *See Jane Win for Girls*, will hopefully inspire your daughter to develop her identity and strengths and help her through these challenging adolescent years. The book provides discussion questions as well, to help keep conversation open between parents and their daughters.

Overweight boys who describe themselves as being slower in their development will need some special support, too. Late-maturing boys often worry about masculinity because they're usually uninterested in girls, and girls are typically not attracted to them because the boys are immature. In the grand scheme of things, these boys may have a great advantage because they have more time to develop interests and activities. However, during adolescence they often feel so misplaced in the mainstream that they suffer painfully. Fathers, big brothers, grandfathers, and uncles are key people in their lives, and mothers need to be particularly careful about not babying their boys, or they will rebel.

Late-maturing boys may be more open to joining gangs and negative peer groups because they are so needy for friends and so determined to prove their machismo. Computers often help them make friends with the advantage of privacy. Although pursuing relationships with computer friends may prevent some loneliness, it doesn't encourage physical activity, which is so important for building self-esteem and a healthy body. Adolescence is an important time for all boys, but especially late-maturing boys, to have male mentors and to become involved in sports, Scouts, or boys' clubs. The late-maturing boy eventually becomes a young man, but not without a fair amount of suffering and feelings of having been left behind.

CHAPTER 7

THE INFLUENCE OF FAMILIES:
How Family Relationships Affect Overweight Children

We've described how overweight children struggle in every aspect of their emotional landscape: with their peers, with their teachers, with their bodies. They struggle in social settings, in the classroom, on the playground, and with their health. But perhaps the most distressing situation of all is at home. Simply put, overweight children tend to have more difficulty with their families than other kids do. So even at home, where we hope an overweight child can find shelter from the taunts of his peers or the prejudice of his teachers and coaches, he tends to feel disconnected and misunderstood.

But it doesn't have to be that way. Families can be a positive influence on children by guiding them toward healthy and active lifestyles and providing them with the nuturance and limits they need. With the findings and conclusions of this chapter, you'll be better prepared take a look at your own family dynamic and modify it as necessary in ways to help your child improve his situation.

PART I—THE FINDINGS

Although many overweight children indicated that they had good family relationships, they were still more likely than average-weight children to indicate that they had poor family relationships (see figures 7.1 and 7.2 on pages 166 and 167). This held true for both girls and boys, although overweight girls indicated even more family problems than overweight boys. My survey found that:

- Very overweight girls are four times more likely, and very overweight boys are three times more likely, to report poor family relationships than their average-weight peers.
- Only a little more than half of very overweight girls (54 percent) and two-thirds of somewhat overweight girls (67 percent) consider their family relationships very good or good, compared with more than three-quarters of the average-weight girls (78 percent).
- Sixty-six percent of the very overweight boys and 78 percent of the somewhat overweight boys have very good or good family relationships, compared with a full 83 percent of the average-weight boys.
- Because interpretations of negative family relationships were worse for the older children (seventh- and eighth-graders) than they were for the younger children (third- and fourth-graders), it can be assumed that family relationships will become worse in high school for overweight children.

FAMILY RELATIONSHIP PROBLEMS

The fact that more overweight children than average-weight children see their family lives as problematic completes the grim cycle of the emotional turmoil for these kids. As we've seen in previous chapters, every factor related to weight—including social and emotional issues, achievement, worries, fears, activities and interests, and developmental problems—has been indicated more frequently as troublesome by overweight children. All those issues trickle down and affect family interactions, which are also aggravated or intensified by negative parent-child relationships. Battles about weight are multiplied by other family skirmishes, and continued family altercations

Figure 7.1
Quality of Family Relationships (Girls), by Weight Category

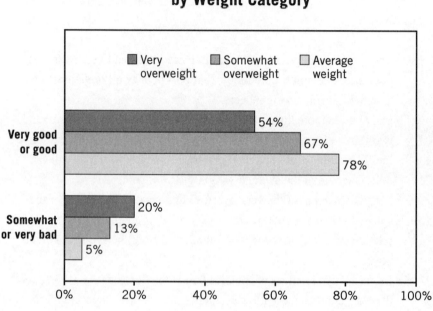

and confusion drive the children they involve to search for love through food. Whether the bone of contention is food or almost anything else, family discord plays itself out through overeating and through family inactivity. The importance of good family relationships was apparent in the interviews of the adults who went on to have happy and healthy lives, which should be encouraging to parents of today's overweight kids. Parents *can* make a difference!

PARENTS ARE GOOD ROLE MODELS

If children view their family relationships as good, they are more likely to see parents as role models, and they are also more likely to be willing to learn from their parents. According to my research, overweight children

Figure 7.2
Quality of Family Relationships (Boys), by Weight Category

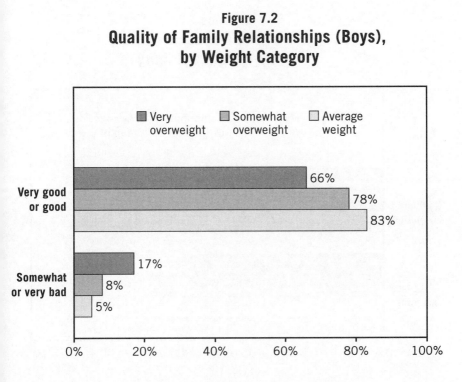

were less likely than average-weight children to indicate their parents as role models (see figures 7.3 and 7.4 on pages 168 and 169). That is, while approximately three-quarters of the average-weight children selected their parents as role models, only a little more than half of the very overweight children made the same choice.

Girls in all weight categories were somewhat more likely to choose their mothers rather than their fathers, probably the result of gender similarity. Furthermore, general emotional adjustment for girls was not dependent on whether they chose mothers or fathers. That is, for many girls, identifying with the opposite-sex parent has encouraged them to become interested in math, science, sports, auto mechanics, or other male-stereotyped interests.

On the other hand, for boys, close identification with mothers and particularly with gender-stereotyped interests of women, often leads to social

Figure 7.3
Parent Role Models (Girls),
by Weight Category

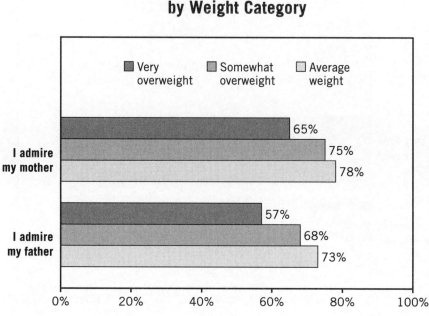

confidence problems. Peer society is more accepting of girls who seem less feminine than of boys who seem too feminine.

My research showed that among the very overweight boys (unlike the other male weight groups), more boys selected their mothers than their fathers as role models by a slight margin.

This is an important finding because when boys choose fathers as role models or even when they believe themselves similar to both parents, they seem to make better social adjustments during adolescence than boys who identify with only their mothers. So good father-son relationships are yet another area where overweight boys are missing out.

Why is this gap occurring? It may be due to the fact that fathers are less accepting of their overweight boys, thus discouraging boys from valuing their relationships with their fathers. Men tend to be less accepting of overweight in others, both when they are boys, as was shown in chapter 3, and when they are men, as shown by these findings.

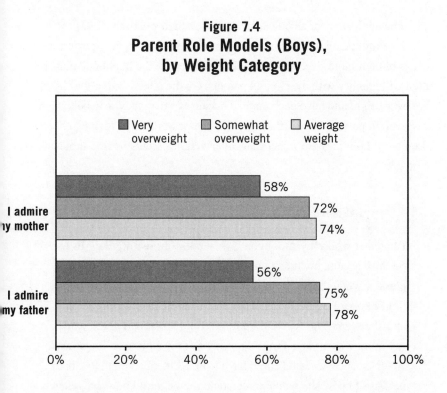

Figure 7.4
Parent Role Models (Boys), by Weight Category

What Influences Children When Choosing Role Models?

Social learning theory research explains that children identify with adults based on three variables. Children are more likely to choose adults as role models if:

• They see similarities between themselves and the adults.

Example: Overweight children might be more likely to see a weight similarity between themselves and a parent who is also overweight, but less likely to see themselves as similar to a thin parent.

• The adults are nurturing and loving toward them.

Example: Parents may unconsciously reject overweight children and not be as nurturing to them as they might be to their thin children. (Many parents have confided their rejecting feelings to me.)

• The adults appear as powerful figures in their children's lives.

Example: Children may consider overweight parents very powerful because of their large size, which may in turn increase the likelihood that children will identify with overweight parents. On the other hand, if the children are overweight and have been taunted because of that, they may believe that overweight parents have little status and are powerless. In such cases, children would be likely to reject their overweight parents as role models, as Ana did.

"I Wished I Could Have a Thin, American Mom"

I hated it when my mom came to school on visiting day. In her Spanish accent, my mom would ask my teacher how I was doing in class. I wanted to talk for her because I was ashamed my mom didn't know English better. Then I'd listen to Tanya's mother talk, and she seemed so much more refined and American. Even worse, my mom was fat and Tanya's mom was thin. I thought Tanya was so lucky, and I wished I could have a thin, American mom to talk to because I knew she would understand me better. I knew that when I grew up and had my own family, I wanted to be like Tanya's mom.

Ana, fifth grade

Girls and boys who reject their parents as role models typically select other adults or peers. Even children who select their parents as role models may choose other role models in addition to their parents. Some of those role models may have an excellent influence, while others may have a negative influence. Overweight girls in my survey were more likely than average-weight girls to choose adult friends and aunts as role models (see figure 7.5). Because they tended not to choose mothers as role models, we can probably assume that at least some of the alternative choices were made because of conflict or misunderstandings between girls and their mothers or because the girls did not see their mothers as powerful enough to be their role models.

While aunts and other adults can be good or bad role models, de-

Figure 7.5
Other Role Models (Girls), by Weight Category

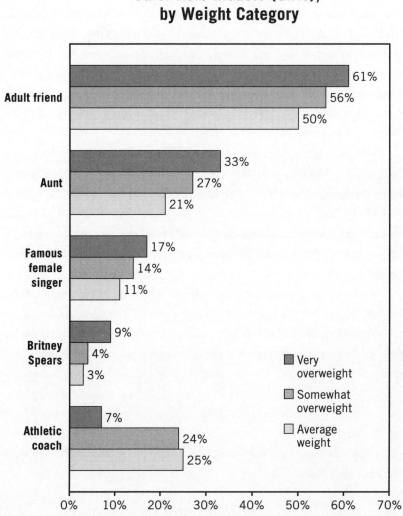

pending on the particular adult, overweight girls, more frequently than average-weight girls, chose famous singers, particularly Britney Spears, as an alternative for female role models. Undoubtedly the girls select such role models partly due to the fantasy allure.

Sharon recalled her own childhood fantasy as an overweight teen. She believed that her weight and emotional problems would disappear if she could become an actress because to her actresses were beautiful, thin, attractive, and financially secure—thus successful and happy. However, this was just her fantasy, and one that unfortunately indicates that their more frequent choice of screen star role models means overweight girls are spending too many hours watching movies and television. In the same vein, the small percentage of very overweight girls who chose coaches as role models reflects their lesser involvement in sports.

As noted above, boys less frequently chose their fathers or mothers as role models. And they were less likely to select other appropriate adults as adult role models as well (see figure 7.6). That is, overweight boys were less likely than average-weight boys to choose athletic coaches as role models, and compared with somewhat overweight or average-weight boys, very overweight boys were also less likely to choose adult friends as role models.

Interestingly, overweight boys were more likely than average-weight boys to choose Boy Scout leaders as role models. Scout leaders may have a very positive and active influence on overweight boys, particularly since heavy boys are less likely than average-weight boys to choose athletic coaches or adult friends. For overweight boys and girls who reject sports, scouting groups can offer active, less competitive alternatives to keep children lively, energized, and interested. Among the successful women from my *See Jane Win* research, many said that Girl Scout leaders had been their role models because they considered them to be powerful women who were ahead of their times.

FAMILY SCENARIOS THAT CAUSE WEIGHTY PROBLEMS

Although no exact family typologies cause children to become overweight, in the adult interviews there emerged some typical parenting scenarios that cultivated children's overweight. The following scenarios highlight the

Figure 7.6
Other Role Models (Boys),
by Weight Category

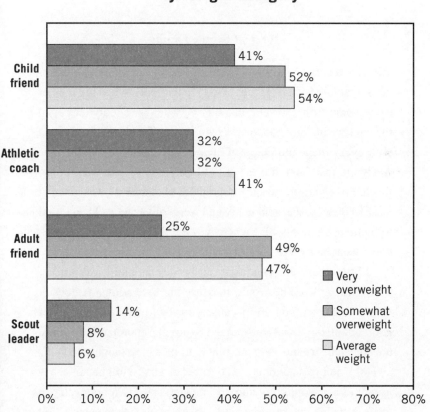

family environments that foster weight problems, but in real life there are many permutations and combinations of these prototypes. Being sensitive to troublesome family patterns can help parents and professionals avoid the pitfalls that prevent healthy and physically fit lifestyles.

The Happy Heavies

Many of the children surveyed and some adult interviewees were part of functional, happy families but were overweight nevertheless. Parents provided reasonably well-balanced meals and knew about good nutrition, but despite that, the entire family ate too much, too often. Members of these so-called Happy Heavy families were more likely to be somewhat overweight, though, rather than obese. Terri's "jolly family" is a perfect example.

Terri's Lovable Family

We were a very social family, and eating was an important part of our social life. Everything revolved around food. When my mother came home from the supermarket, we would excitedly tear open the bags to find any goodies. We ate healthy foods, but drank soda with every meal and between meals. My mother cooked, so we rarely ate fast food, but the quantity of food we ate was far too much. For example, instead of 4 ounces of chicken, I was given at least 10 ounces. We ate quickly and were jolly eaters. Once, I tried to figure out a family plan where we could all lose weight, but that never went anywhere because eating was so much fun.

My mother had been heavy all her life and still was while I was growing up. She would reassure me by saying, "It doesn't matter what size you are because you look nice and have other good qualities." I was surrounded by loving grandparents, aunts, uncles, adult friends, and a brother, all of whom taught me skills and told me I was adorable and talented and had a bright smile. My grandmother would hug and kiss me and say, "Oh, honey, try to lose a little weight, but first have a piece of chocolate cake." I felt very loved, and my relatives wouldn't dare let my self-esteem slip despite my being overweight.

Terri, adult interviewee

Ralph also came from a Happy Heavy family. He described some of his family members as chunky or chubby and others as thin, and he didn't remember his parents ever telling him what to eat or not eat. In fact, he ate too much, and his mother always prepared plenty of his favorite foods for him. He especially remembered bacon and fried veal sandwiches for lunch.

At first his weight didn't bother him because he felt confident and had good family relations. He later became aware of his overweight problem in high school, and in college he finally became conscious of changing his diet and eating healthier. His family never changed their happy eating plan. Like Terri's family, they simply ate too much.

Another Happy Heavy family member was Jeff. When Jeff was 12 years old, his doctor told him to lose weight, and prescribed diet pills and an appropriate diet for him to follow. The doctor described Jeff as being 70 pounds overweight. His parents prepared plenty of healthy food; however, to lose weight, he needed to eat much less. Jeff told me that if he had lived in a different family, he probably would have been 20 pounds lighter. You may notice that Jeff had awareness of his family's role, yet didn't blame all his overweight on his family's eating environment.

Characteristics of the Happy Heavies are a good quality of life, healthy but not necessarily active interests, and supportive family members. Thus, these children tended to have good self-confidence, although they weren't taught to set limits on their eating. The interviewed adults who came from Happy Heavy families had the best chance of reaching a healthy weight because other important components of family life had been mentally healthy. Thus, for those of you who have supportive families, the transition from a Happy Heavy to a Happy Healthy family (as is detailed in "Rescuing Techniques" on page 184) will not be as difficult.

The Lonely Health Nut

This dysfunctional family relationship includes one parent who is overly concerned about nutrition and exercise, either because the parent is healthfully thin or because the parent struggled with overweight and continues to be health conscious in adulthood. The Lonely Health Nut parent may be very controlling in guiding children, or may only be exasperated by both the other parent's laissez-faire attitude and the children's disrespect for guidelines. The other parent sabotages the first parent's nutrition control by sneaking food to the children and secretly providing snacks that the other parent has forbidden. Parents will argue about food, and the children are likely to become manipulative and rebellious while dealing with serious weight and nutrition problems. Gail's family is an example of how serious these struggles can become.

My Dad Didn't Want a Fat Wife or Fat Daughters

My father was a health nut. He would eat wheat germ and ice milk and would never let us have ice cream or candy. I was the youngest of five girls, and all of us, as well as my mother, were overweight. My dad was thin and didn't want a fat wife or fat daughters. There were constant weight battles, and my mom would win us over with "Bad daddy, I'm a great mommy. I'll give you food, but don't tell your father."

I felt bad about my weight, but in the frustration of it I would eat the things that would make my father crazy. Pretty soon I started hidden binge eating to compensate for the missing hugs and love that Daddy didn't give us girls because we were all fat. My sisters did the same. After my dad died, we were going through his possessions and discovered that in his diary he kept records of our weight. There it was: Gail 170 pounds, Dawn 185 pounds, and so on. We never realized how our weight games controlled our dad's life and how desperate he was to control our eating. All of us were obsessed with food and in a battle with our father.

Gail, adult interviewee

Samantha's mother, Jane, was the Lonely Health Nut in her family. Jane had been overweight as a child and dealt with adolescent bulimia. As an adult she maintained a healthy weight, but she was not a healthy eater. She worked hard in an important professional position, so she had little time for meal preparation. Her husband, John, who worked part-time, was the home-maker and cared for 6-year-old Samantha. Although John cooked dinner, Jane desperately wanted to control Samantha's eating. John, who had never had weight problems, wanted to let his daughter eat whatever she liked.

Jane would make the rules and John would break them; he sabotaged Jane's nutrition plans regularly.

Because Jane had struggled with her own weight problems, she identified closely with her daughter and felt certain that Samantha would become overweight also. At first Jane tried to be kind and patient with setting eating limits for Samantha, but Samantha knew she could ignore those limits by getting snacks from her dad. Samantha became a rapid and surreptitious eater so her mother wouldn't catch her eating "disallowed" foods. She was also disrespectful and defiant toward Jane. Jane found herself both loving and hating her daughter because she feared that her daughter would experience the same horrendous eating disorders she had experienced. Jane admitted she wasn't a very good role model for Samantha's eating, and food was a constant family battle.

Eventually, Jane and John divorced. Samantha is now living in two homes and manipulating both parents through food. There is not a healthy, happy outlook for Samantha's future, despite the fact that both her parents love her very much. Jane would have benefited from further therapy to deal with her fears about her daughter's weight gain, as well as her own imbalanced eating. John and Jane's food battles were only part of a larger struggle that went unsolved.

Phyllis's parents' differences were less extreme than those of Gail's or Samantha's parents, but they caused her problems nevertheless. Her dad had been obese as a child and had been ridiculed by his parents, but he eventually reached a healthy adult weight. Because he had suffered abuse about his weight, he was eager to prevent his daughter from suffering the same fate. He wasn't cruel, but he did anxiously and continually reprimand Phyllis: "You shouldn't be eating this" and "You don't want to get fat, do you?" Although she knew he meant well and loved her, his comments hurt Phyllis emotionally and didn't encourage her to lose weight. Instead, his anxiety made her feel more anxious, and thus she turned to food. She ate constantly almost to spite her father.

Phyllis's mother didn't actually sabotage her father's efforts, but showed confidence that Phyllis would figure it out on her own. She would say encouragingly, "I believe you'll do this when you're ready, when you realize what you need to do." Phyllis liked her mother's approach better and interpreted it as respect and confidence in her. Between seventh and eighth grades, Phyllis lost 70 pounds by joining an adolescent Weight Watchers group. She believed that her mother's support helped her to make the decision to lose weight, and she has managed to keep her healthy weight, nutrition, and exercise routines as an adult.

In some cases, a grandparent can occupy the role of Lonely Health Nut by giving constant advice about healthy food, while the parents resist the good advice because they feel too controlled. This is unlikely to cause as much dysfunction in the family as it does when a parent is the Lonely Health Nut, but parents may oppose the grandparent's control by resisting teaching their children about healthy eating. There likely will be angry feelings among grandparents, parents, and children.

The Family Scapegoat

A surprisingly frequent pattern in families is the lone fat child—the sitting duck and scapegoat for all the family problems. Doreen, Patti, Nancy, Sally, Nina, and Gabi were the fat kids in their families. Their families could snack, devour, guzzle, gorge, and tuck away as much food and drink as they chose while reminding the fatties that they better not eat so much. Moms could fry, bake, and serve fatty meats and rich sauces, cheesecakes, and pie à la mode. While everyone was eating up and not gaining weight, the overweight ones would sneak their share and still gain the ugly pounds. When a child is a Family Scapegoat, usually the family has other problems that are being overlooked, with undeserved blame directed at the overweight child.

Doreen described the plentiful cakes, pies, and ice cream served in her home, paired with admonitions not to gain weight. Patti's mom provided the money for candy treats, and her dad prepared Sunday-night sundaes and root beer floats. Nancy's thin mom and sister commented, "Don't eat the starchy stuff" and "Don't eat the Snickers bars," as the mom served starchy foods for dinner and Snickers bars for dessert. Her mom and sister would indulge themselves, but Nancy was expected to abstain from treats because she was the fat one in the family. Ironically, when Nancy lost weight in high school, the family arguments and scapegoating continued, only with a different message: "You'd better eat some food or you'll starve" or, even worse, "You'll probably gain the weight back anyway, so you might as well eat." Nancy didn't gain the weight back, but the family taunting hurt. Fortunately, she had gained enough confidence through her success to continue to eat moderately and nutritiously.

In Nancy's family there may have been an underlying dynamic based on her older sister's wishing to share power with their single mother. In single-parent homes, it is not unusual for the mother or father to "adultize" an oldest child by planning together and sharing adult secrets as if the child were another adult. In many ways this intergenerational relationship is insecure for both parent and child. The parent is aware that the child must grow up, become independent, and probably marry. The child is unconsciously aware that the adult status is precarious. Mother and older child feel closer as they talk about the problems of the younger child. The scapegoat thus provides the glue that cements the relationship between the older child and the parent. It is obvious to the outsider that this scapegoating relationship is dysfunctional to all, but for the parent and older child, the scapegoat is always there to keep them feeling close together.

Sally's story added another nuance. Her parents adopted her and they were both very thin. They ate whatever they wanted even if it wasn't particularly healthful, and neither of them exercised. They gorged on pasta, sauces, and gravies and didn't seem to gain an ounce, while Sally shared the same menus and gained weight. Many families just find it easier and delicious to serve junk food to all, and there's plenty of advertising to make this unhealthy food attractive.

Nina's family did little exercise, and all were picky eaters. Nina's mother would make four different meals for supper just to please everyone. But she wasn't a very good cook, so sometimes they were only individualized TV dinners. Nina's weight problem was ignored, and she felt isolated from her family.

Like our other Family Scapegoats, Gabi was the only one in the family with a weight problem. The family never exercised, but they were certainly concerned about Gabi's weight. There was no junk food in their house, so

Gabi would go to her friends' homes and enjoy wolfing down snacks there. Once a year her family would visit Gabi's aunt, uncle, and cousins in Florida. Her thin cousins were active in sports, so Gabi dreaded when her uncle routinely weighed each child in the family and announced the weights to everyone. Only Gabi would get the same warnings every year from her uncle: "Don't eat junk food," "Eat healthy," "Be sure to exercise." Although her parents never teased her, and the rest of the family didn't laugh or make fun of her, she was humiliated by the comparison of her weight with those of her cousins. While Gabi's cousins may have felt good, healthy, and confident by the comparison, Gabi became the Family Scapegoat for the entire extended family.

Despite their pain, most of the women who were Family Scapegoats learned to take control of their eating and lose weight, but each had an extraordinary struggle. As you recall their detailed stories from the earlier chapters, often a defining moment or a significant person who believed in them empowered them to make positive changes in their lifestyles. And while the scapegoating continued, they rose above the family situation and on to success outside their home lives.

The Perfectionists

Perfectionistic families can actually encourage children to become overweight because children who feel like nothing they do is good enough to please their parents can easily give up on themselves and eat for comfort. Parents who constantly praise children's appearances with "You're a beauty," "You're gorgeous," or "You're perfect" set kids up for feeling pressure to have all the qualities they're praised for. These children become dependent on praise, avoid activities they aren't the best at, and struggle with feelings of failure when they aren't the prettiest or the thinnest.

Lorie worried about being too fat by the time she was 4, even though she wasn't overweight. The childhood picture she showed me was proof of that. Lorie's older sister had an eating disorder and other extended family members had weight problems, so there must have been plenty of family talk about weight to make Lorie so concerned about her appearance.

Being overweight in elementary school made Lorie miserable and lonely.

She withdrew from all her activities because as a perfectionist she was afraid to fail. Now that Lorie's an adult, she has her weight under control and plays sports and exercises, although she still struggles with perfectionism and with believing she's thin enough. I noticed she wore a baggy shirt for our interview, although there was no overweight to cover up now. Lorie is anxious not to pass her perfectionism or her weight problems on to her baby daughter. With her new insight on how overpraising appearance can lead to weight pressures, as well as her knowledge about nutrition and exercise, she hopes her little girl will grow to be healthy and fit but won't need to feel perfect to be happy. Teaching children early that they can be good at and enjoy activities without having to be the best should be an early priority. Also, letting them know that they are more than just a pretty face and a thin figure is important communication in a world where the media shouts otherwise.

3D Families: Depressed, Dependent, and Down-and-Out

More obese and very overweight children tend to be from 3D Families—families that are depressed, dependent, and down-and-out. Overweight children who described themselves as having very poor family relationships may have families who are struggling with many other issues besides overweight. Illness, death of a family member, divorce, or single parenting may be overwhelming issues in 3D Families. Fast food may be a substitute for meals, and snacking and junk food may predominate. Often, parents can't find the time or the energy for meal preparation and may not be sensitive to nutrition issues. Children eat in front of the television alone or with the family, and social family interchange revolves around what's on TV that night. Children may spend more time at home alone as latchkey kids because parents may not be able to afford after-school care. Game playing, sports activities, and school learning take a backseat to three other Ds in 3D Family homes: dining, drinking, and desperation.

Susan, Darlene, and Alex struggled in 3D Families for at least part of childhood. From Susan's point of view, her mother worked most of the time and was not home much. Her dad cooked for her, but whether Susan ate alone (most of the time) or with him (some of the time), it was always in front of the TV. She had no siblings and very few friends. Even though she feared her dad because he was so strict, his suicide when she was a high school student left her grieving and desperately lonely. She consoled herself with food and found a boyfriend not only to cheer her up, but also to overeat with her. Susan gained 100 pounds over the next year. Gorging on food was the center of her life and soothed her sadness, and it left her little time for developing interests or talents. She was never active in school, the community, or physical activities.

Darlene, too, had a 3D Family. Her mother died of cancer when Darlene was only 4, so she felt different and deprived not only because of her weight but also because she was brought up by a single father. In Darlene's case, other family members could support her. She developed her artistic talents and made some very good friends. Despite that, she experienced many difficult, sad, and unhealthy years. Darlene's story illustrates how family members can pitch in to help a niece, nephew, or grandchild and make an extraordinary difference.

Dad Was Clueless

My dad raised me with "benign neglect." He would go to work, come home, make dinner for me, and go to sleep. He was depressed, and he had no idea what I was doing or eating. I did no exercise and fed my sorrows with carbohydrates. For a little while I lived with my aunt, and she took care of me and put me on a diet. I lost some weight during that time and felt good about myself. Then I went back to living with my dad, eating for comfort again, and put the weight back on. My dad loved me, but he was clueless as to how to guide me, and I desperately needed limits.

Darlene, adult interviewee

The childhood of sixth-grader Alex, described in chapter 3, was also one with very few limits. He was the only child of a single mother who struggled with other issues as well as overweight. She helped Alex to feel loved, but never taught him to respect boundaries and actually joined him in denial of his overweight. Thus, Alex's self-control problems extended beyond food to his behavior and school achievement.

A 3D Family rarely finds the energy or the confidence to provide appropriate nutritional or activity guidance for their children. Unless there is outside intervention, children from 3D Families are often destined to continue growing toward morbid obesity. Outside intervention may be spontaneous and come from important and caring people in a child's life, as in Susan's and Darlene's cases. A teacher or psychologist could help a desperate, overweight child find support and guidance as well.

FAMILY SIBLING SAGAS

Family sibling sagas can take place in any family. It is no coincidence that in my clinical work I frequently discover great variety in the eating habits of siblings. When one child is a picky eater, the other eats voraciously. If one is willing to try everything, another seems to like almost nothing. While parents often assume that these differences are caused by genetics (and indeed genetic issues may play a part), competition for parents' attention often differentiates siblings' eating habits. Children always compete for parents' attention, and eating is only one way this competition plays out. Siblings also compete over academic grades, creativity, athletic skill, organization, or fast or slow pace. Anything that helps a child capture adult attention from other siblings is fair game for rivalry.

Amanda provided a crystal clear example of how sibling rivalry affects appetites. Amanda was always very active, but despite her high activity level, she was very heavy. Even when she did hard-core running and basketball drills for 3 hours a day, she remained overweight because she consumed too much food. She noshed on junk food, often eating an entire bag of chips while watching a movie. She devoured Southern-style, calorie-laden fried foods. She wondered where and why all that food consumption started, and traced it back to her little brother, who never wanted to eat. She remembered her parents' desperate cries of "Why won't you eat?" and "You have to eat something," and then Amanda's proud comments of "Look, Mom—I cleaned my plate!" Amanda felt like it was an achievement and a competitive accomplishment to not only eat, but eat the most. As Amanda said, "Being a good eater was a way for me to get positive attention from my mom."

Harry was also a competitive eater, but that's because it was a survival skill for him. In his family of nine, there was a race to get one of the 12 pieces of chicken for dinner, and if he ate fast enough, he might even have two. Harry's competitive eating habits changed when his older brothers left home and there was considerably more food to share. And by that time his dad was suffering from a heart problem, so his parents had become much more health conscious. His parents no longer stocked their home with sweets, and Harry adjusted well to the more nutritious meals.

Within the various family scenarios described, sibling issues often raised their competitive heads. For example, when Nancy would go bike riding with her sister, her sister would chastise her for not being able to keep up. Plus, Nancy's sister was thin and had never had to worry about a weight problem; even so, she managed to join with her mother in nagging Nancy about what she ate. Recognizing that sibling rivalry often plays at least a small part in children's eating can help parents guide children with individual differences toward healthy, appropriate eating habits. Perhaps fewer mealtime comments about the "poor, starving children in Africa," along with reducing the "You'll get fat" or "You'd better clean your plate" comments, can smooth out the heavy-versus-light sibling differences and prevent any child's weight from becoming the center of attention.

PART II—RESCUING TECHNIQUES

Parents can change many of the family dynamics that perpetuate unhealthy lifestyles, although changing family interactions is never easy because they continue by inertia and may even be hold-over habits from the parents' childhoods. On the other hand, conscious change is always possible, as our success stories confirm. This section will help you to:

- Develop family role models
- Change Happy Heavies to Happy Healthies
- Create fitness through team parenting
- Eliminate scapegoats by including the whole family

• Set high expectations without perfectionism
• Raise family grades from 3Ds to 3Cs
• Stabilize sibling solidarity

FAMILY ROLE MODELS

Knowing how children are influenced to select role models can help you guide your children toward finding appropriate ones. You will recall that children tend to identify with adults who are nurturing, have characteristics similar to theirs, and are powerful figures. Your efforts at demonstrating that you care can cause your child to feel more nurtured by you. Preserving some time to be alone with your child will also convey this. Pointing out similarities between your childhood and your child's experiences can also influence your child to consider you a role model. For example, comparing your similarities and interests in art, music, biking, or cooking can unite the two of you. You can also note how similar your child is to your spouse, an aunt, an uncle, a grandparent, or an adult friend you admire, thereby encouraging your child to consider them as a role model. Comparing characteristics you see in your child with those of a scientist, teacher, artist, or musician can also encourage your child's selection of positive role models.

The more confident you feel as a parent and an adult, the more likely your children will see you as a powerful person. All parents lose confidence and feel overwhelmed sometimes, but that's a secret you can keep from your children until they're older. For now, even when you don't feel in charge, pretend you do. Acting self-assured will make you feel more confident, and it will be a positive influence on your children as well. You can also empower other family members by making positive comments about them to your children. If you compliment your spouse or your children's grandparents, your children will be more likely to want to be like them. But turnabout is fair play, so it would be better for all if your partner or parent has good words to say about your wisdom as well. Your children will admire you and hope they can grow up to be as wonderful as you are, which gives you opportunities to pass on healthy values to them.

When You Prefer Your Child
Not Select a Particular Role Model

There may be adults and kids in your child's life that you'd rather your child didn't admire. Some people who are not good role models for young children are alcoholic or violent parents, negative or angry grandparents, wild or defiant peers, or obnoxious neighbors.

If your child is attracted to poor role models, be sure not to unconsciously encourage his bad choices. Even if there's a divorce and you no longer respect your former spouse, don't tell your child when he loses his temper that he reminds you of his angry father. It would also be better not to describe your former wife as "having all the money" and not sharing it with you. That may be factual, but it will tempt your children to defend that parent, thus making them side with the other parent.

Likewise, when you tell your daughter she's acting just like the trampy girls she hangs around with, you're inadvertently saying she belongs with the crowd of kids you'd prefer she stayed away from. Pointing out similarities or power between your children and negative role models serves to attract your children to them. This happens much more frequently than you would believe.

FROM HAPPY HEAVIES
TO HAPPY HEALTHIES

A medical crisis is often the defining event that converts a Happy Heavy family from a life of denial to a commitment to healthy eating and lifestyle activities. But there's no reason for your family to wait for a crisis to initiate the changes required to become healthier. Earlier, we alerted you to the grave consequences of overweight for you and your children's overall health (see chapter 2). Overeating and lack of exercise prevents your family members from living long and happy lives. The sooner you modify the family's unhealthy lifestyle, the more likely you are to extend the healthy and vital years of your family's lives. Your reading this book shows that you are not in denial of your family's overweight problem. If you already live in a family where your relationships are reasonably good, you need only to redefine your eating and exercise patterns.

A Family Meeting

If your children are beyond preschool age, and certainly if they are adolescents, a family meeting to design a healthy meal and activity plan will encourage commitment from the entire family. If any of your children are resistant or still in denial of their weight problems, express your confidence that they'll eventually see the benefit of this change, and ask that they at least not interfere with the family's efforts. At the meeting your family can decide whether tracking weight loss on a chart will be helpful. Children may feel too pressured and competitive with a family weight loss chart, so it may be best for each family member to keep a private record. An accurate bathroom scale helps to keep track of everyone's progress.

Changing from Family Feast to Family Famine

Of course, you won't have to go to the extreme of famine, but it may feel like famine to families accustomed to eating far too much. Slowing the pace of eating and not prolonging mealtime will go a long way toward cutting caloric intake. Serving portions that are half of what you'd normally eat and substituting extra vegetables will help the family reach satiety sooner while promoting healthy eating. You can control portion size by preparing plates in the kitchen, rather than passing the food around the table.

Here are some other concrete changes you can make.

• *Talk and walk.* Instead of socializing over food, transfer family discussions from the table to the outdoors. Talking while walking will permit the happy conversations to continue through daily activity. One research study showed that daily walking, with no change in diet, caused women to lose 7 percent of their abdominal fat and an average of 3 pounds within a year. You might say that's not much weight, but the experimental group did not change their diets or add other exercise. Imagine what might happen if you did. Family bicycle rides, table tennis games, aerobic workouts, swims, jogs, and hikes can be daily or at least weekend events, depending on the weather and family interest. The fun and laughter of your jolly mealtimes can now be part of your activities and help you burn calories as well.

- *Make grocery shopping changes.* You will want to spend more time and money in the produce, fish, and meat departments than in the soft drink, bakery, and snack aisles. Bringing home healthy foods rather than unhealthy snacks will go a long way toward maintaining healthy eating patterns for the whole family. Keeping junk food out of the house will help everyone resist temptation. Occasional treats are still encouraged, though, so your family doesn't feel deprived.
- *Get nutritional guidance.* Often, families who eat too much by habit require professional guidance for meal planning. Your family physician can recommend a nutritionist, or you may want to purchase a nutrition handbook to help you with portion size and balanced meals. Many cookbooks are specifically designed for those who are concerned about family weight gain. Family meals can still be delicious, more nutritious, and less fattening.

TEAM-PARENTING FITNESS

To erase the Lonely Health Nut family scenario, you will have to take a look at all the adults who are caring for your children. Mothers, fathers, grandparents, nannies, day care center staff, and family day care providers all affect children's eating and activity levels. Parents should take the responsibility of communicating to child care providers, whether they be family members or professionals in a day care setting, about their concerns for healthy eating and exercise.

Avoid Extremes

Whether you're communicating to a spouse, your adult children, or an institution, if you are too extreme or too rigid in your demands, you will soon gain the reputation of being a "health nut." Overweight or not, children don't require rigidity to be healthy. Unless children have allergies to foods, your directions about eating and exercise can be general enough so the person responsible for following your directions doesn't feel totally controlled by you. If you are overly controlling, your food and exercise plans will likely be undermined and ignored.

If you believe that your spouse or parent is subverting your strategies for healthy nutrition, try to put aside your anxiety about your children's weight and agree to a compromise about what your children should eat. For example, Jane could have agreed with John to let Samantha have dessert once a day or an occasional bag of chips. And John might have been willing to go along with encouraging healthy veggie or fruit snacks at other times.

Grandparents should also be allowed to openly give their grandchildren treats on occasion. If they can't, they will surreptitiously overindulge their grandchildren more frequently, and that will not be good for the children either. It's also disrespectful to the parents and will hurt family relationships.

Make Exercise Fun

As to the exercise component, Lonely Health Nut parents will feel less lonely if they convince children to participate in activities that are fun as well as forms of exercise. It is important for the saboteur to compromise and get involved as well. If parents are active together, it can make a huge difference. Sometimes giving a bicycle or roller skates as a gift for a birthday, Christmas, or Chanukah can initiate a new exercise interest. Joining a Y or a fitness center can also make exercise seem fun and not a punishment.

Find a Mediator

A nutritionist, family doctor, or psychologist can help mediate a family health plan that feels like a compromise to both parents. Within the safety of a confidential office, parents are often willing to express how overcontrolled they feel by one parent's rigid orders or how frustrated they feel by the other parent's unhealthy undermining. Just talking about the issue and acknowledging that children's health should be prioritized over adult power struggles can decrease the tension and the sabotage and bring parents and parenting teams together for more collaborative and moderate healthy eating and exercise. If you consider that giving and withdrawing food are often tied to feelings of giving and withdrawing love, you can better understand why these scenarios are so common and so difficult to resolve.

NO MORE SCAPEGOATS

Ending the scapegoating by including all children is the vital first step to encouraging children to be healthy eaters. Making one child into a Family Scapegoat doesn't typically happen intentionally, but it continues because it cements other family relationships. Family members draw closer together when they make one person in a family bear the blame for other people's problems. And this bonding—whether the scapegoat is an alcoholic, a drug addict, the problem child, or too fat—is dramatically resistant to change. However, a designated scapegoat in the family indicates a family problem, so if you recognize this scenario in your family, I suggest you get some family counseling. You may require more help than I can offer you here, but the scenarios I describe below may help you get started fixing the family dynamic.

An Unsatisfactory Spousal Relationship

When parents have problems within their relationship, one or both may unconsciously blame a child for the problems. Thus, disputes that the adults can't resolve may be projected onto the Family Scapegoat, and the child's problem becomes the one that attracts blame. Sometimes the only close and agreeable discussions parents can have surround the problems of the scapegoat child. For example, a mother who feels sexually rejected by her husband might find herself serving her daughter too much food while also scolding her for overeating. Thus, the mother can blame her own overweight on genetics because her daughter is also overweight. She also protects herself from feeling jealous of her husband's special treatment of her daughter and can talk intimately to her husband, but only when they worry together about their daughter's overweight. The husband may resent his wife's weight and feel unable to talk to her about it directly, but he can at least caution her to monitor their daughter's weight, hoping that his wife will also take the advice. Parents can prevent this type of situation by working on their marriage and handling problems without making their child the fall guy for their issues.

A Missing Adult Relationship

When a single parent is raising a family or a spouse travels a great deal, a lonely or single parent may develop a close, adultlike relationship with one of the children, usually the oldest. The bond that holds that relationship together may exclude other children in the family, who may be scapegoated either for overweight or behavior problems. If a parent notices that most conversations with the child confidant concern the problems of other children in the family, the parent should redirect the conversation by sharing the child's interests, developing activities together that include all the children, and refusing to talk only about the Family Scapegoat's problems.

Don't be surprised if it is difficult to redirect your time spent with the child confidant. The child looks forward to joining you in conversations about a sibling's problems and will return to the subject because it makes the confidant feel like a good and powerful child. You'll need to remember to admonish your confidant by saying something like "We won't talk about Nancy now. She seems to be doing quite well. Let's talk about the party you went to last night." I used Nancy as an example because you will remember how her single mother and sister continued to scapegoat her, first for being overweight and later for losing too much weight.

SETTING HIGH EXPECTATIONS WITHOUT PERFECTIONISM

Perfectionism has long been considered an underlying cause of eating disorders such as bulimia and anorexia, but it has been targeted less often as a reason for obesity. Yet overweight children may be perfectionists who have given up on bodies that they believe can't be perfected. If perfectionism is an underlying issue for overweight children, there will likely be other problems, like underachievement in school, procrastination, dropping out of activities they aren't best at, and even depression. Here are some suggestions for dealing with perfectionists who also have weight problems.

- Help kids understand that they can feel satisfied when they've done *their* best, not necessarily *the* best. Praise that is enthusiastic but more moderate conveys values that children can achieve. For example, "excellent" is better than "perfect," and "You're a good thinker" is better than "You're brilliant." Also avoid comparative praise such as "You're the best" because it makes kids think they must be the best to satisfy you.
- Explain to children that they may not be learning even if all of their work in school is perfect. Help them understand that mistakes and challenges are an important part of learning. Similar to the example of not being a perfect student, also explain that no one has a perfect body, but a good, healthy body is most important.
- Teach appropriate self-evaluation, and encourage children to learn to accept criticism from adults and other students. Explain that they can learn from the recommendations of others.
- Read biographies together that demonstrate how successful people experienced and learned from failures. Emphasize people's failures and rejections, as well as their successes, and help children to identify with their feelings. Stories from my book *How Jane Won* will be helpful for discussion.
- Don't complain about your own figure or being overweight. Instead, eat healthy, stay active, and accept your own body.
- Share your own mistakes, and model the lessons you learned from them. Talk to yourself aloud about learning from your mistakes so children understand your thinking. Don't be too hard on yourself.
- Help children to laugh at their mistakes. Humor helps perfectionists.
- Show children how to congratulate others on their successes. They will feel they are coping better with competition as they congratulate others.
- Teach children routines, habits, and organization. At the same time, it's

important to help them understand that their habits should not be so rigid that they can't change them.

- Purposely break routines so your children are not enslaved by them. For example, if they make their beds daily, permit them to skip the chore on a day when you're in a hurry. If you read to them each night, insist they go to sleep without reading once in a while. Occasional breaks in routines will model flexibility and prevent them from becoming compulsive about habits.

- Teach children creative problem-solving strategies. Brainstorming for ideas that will keep their self-criticism from interfering with their productivity is good.

- Explain to children that there is more than one correct way to do most everything.

- Emphasize that effort counts. If your child is an underachiever and avoids effort because he fears not achieving perfection, help him to gradually increase his effort and show him how that relates to his progress.

- If your child is a high achiever but overstudies for fear of not receiving an A plus, help her to gradually study a little less to show her it will affect her grades only a little. Help her to feel satisfied with a reasonable amount of studying. She needs to balance work with fun.

- Be a role model of healthy excellence. Take pride in the quality of your work, but don't hide your mistakes or criticize yourself constantly. Congratulate yourself when you've done a good job, and let your children know that your own accomplishments give you satisfaction. Don't be a workaholic; you, too, need to have some fun and relaxation. Just for the fun of it, participate in physical activities that you're not very good at. Don't constantly criticize your weight or your appearance.

- Seek professional psychological help for your child and your family if your child's perfectionism is out of control. Perfectionism prevents accomplishments and may cause symptoms of anxiety like stomachaches, headaches, sleeping problems, isolation from peers, or eating too much or too little.

RAISING FAMILY GRADES
FROM 3DS TO 3CS

Changing 3D Families (Depressed, Dependent, and Down-and-Out) to 3C Families (Cheerful, Cooperative, and Creative) goes far beyond the mission of this book. 3D Families require serious outside interventions, like job training and family psychological services. However, changing the lives of children in the family is potentially doable. Many children in 3D Families are able to escape the down-and-out status of their families to achieve health and happiness. Parents, professionals, and friends can be instrumental in helping children raise their own life grades and lower their weight despite a sad, negative, and unhealthy family environment.

Empowering a Child

Believing in a child's ability to change her lifestyle and offering to be a coach or mentor to a child may initiate his escape from overweight, dependency, and despondency to healthy weight, cheer, and creativity. Empowerment usually begins with a private, loving message by letting the child know that you believe that his life can get better. Because children who don't have control over their eating often feel like failures in many ways, it's good to begin an empowering conversation by pointing out a child's strengths. Qualities such as kindness and consideration, or special talents related to school, religion, sports, or arts, may encourage children to realize their capabilities. You can also explain to your child that his being overweight can drag him down and make him feel incapable in many areas.

Parents can support children by developing a nutritional menu that will help them eat healthfully. If you're a teacher or other professional, you may be able to suggest a nurse or nutritionist who can help children eat healthfully despite their family's poor eating habits. Either way, a weight loss group like Weight Watchers for adolescents might provide them with important peer support. A counseling group within a school is also an excellent alternative for children who don't have family support. Group members may finally find peer and adult support for their mission, and weight loss can then feel possible.

Finding Support

The support of a mentor, a Big Sister, or a Big Brother can go a long way toward cheering a forlorn child. An aunt, uncle, or grandparent may also give hope to a child who is surrounded by hopelessness. Recall Darlene's aunt, who helped her after her mother had died and her dad slipped into depression. A local Y or a Girls and Boys Club may be pivotal in offering children a place to exercise, take classes, and develop interests and confidence. Encourage children to read biographies of people whose lives began in poverty or sadness; these can often be inspiring, whether or not the subject had weight problems.

A part-time job may also help a teen find hope for the future. Success in any one area may generalize to confidence in the health area as well because it gives a child a feeling of control over her life. In order for her to move from depression to cheerfulness, she may require medical or psychological intervention, for her weight as well as for her self-concept development.

SIBLING SOLIDARITY

Although sibling rivalry can never be completely eliminated, it can be diminished and at least not be centered on food or exercise. Labeling one child the good eater and the other the picky eater, one child the athlete and the other the klutz, or one child the skinny kid and the other the chubby one can help worsen sibling rivalry and cause overweight children to eat gluttonously, avoid exercise, and feel bad about themselves, and ugly.

Avoiding Food Power Struggles

It's often difficult not to engage in food struggles when children eat too little or too much, but it's best to keep conversation directed to other issues at the table. In addition to providing healthy meals, being good role models for healthy eating will help diminish the struggles. Children need some education about balanced eating with you as the educator, but they don't need battles. If there are differences between parents about eating habits, be sure to discuss those privately and to stay united at mealtime. This holds true as well for grandparents who share family meals.

Exercise for All

While some children in the family may be more successful at sports than others, the mandate for family health should be exercise for all. We've suggested ways to get your family moving, and as long as everyone knows they're expected to be physically active, you can help them find an activity of their choice (see chapter 5). Their power to choose is only in regard to which physical activities they'd like to participate in, not whether they wish to participate at all.

Jealousy Is Not Lethal

Jealousy isn't lethal; it's a natural feeling. It will help if your children are able to express their feelings instead of assuming they are bad for feeling jealous. Just knowing they can express themselves will help them cope. Teaching children to admire and congratulate their siblings at sporting events or concerts also seems to make them feel better. Cheering for other family members encourages them to hope that their family members will also cheer them on—and indeed, for many of my success story interviewees, supportive sisters or brothers made a difference in their courage to lose weight healthfully. Just as there can be a whole smart family, there can also be a whole healthy and physically fit family.

CHAPTER 8

THE SIX-STEP
HEALTHY RESCUE PLAN:
How You Can Help Your Child

Think about what you'd like for your children. Most parents want their children to be happy, healthy, and self-confident. They would like their children to find satisfying careers and life partners who love and respect them, or at least find a group of close, supportive friends.

These basic goals certainly seem attainable and reasonable. And yet, for no other reason than the "crime" of being overweight, these goals seem unattainable for many children. Being overweight brings more attention to children's weaknesses and makes their strengths and talents seem almost invisible. All the world sees is a kid with a weight problem. It's not fair, and it doesn't have to remain that way. Your child, like all children, deserves the opportunity to achieve his dreams.

By now, as you've read the in-depth descriptions of what these children are going through, it's no surprise if you feel a little overwhelmed. You may even feel that you've already gone down the wrong path and contributed to your child's grief.

But one thing you shouldn't feel is powerless to change your relationship with your child. Even if you're hesitant to begin the rescue plan because it's too late or will worsen your relationship with your children or partner, I urge you to consider that this chapter may be the most important one you ever read about your child. By now, I hope you realize your child's problem will not just magically disappear. And that you have a role in helping turn the corner to a healthier, happier life full of all the best things you want for your child. With the Six-Step Healthy Rescue Plan that follows, I'll show you how to figure out where and how to start your intervention to help end your child's sad cycle of obesity. This framework will help you organize and prioritize your use of the rescue techniques you've read about in the earlier chapters of this book.

The Six-Step Healthy Rescue Plan will start you on the path to rescuing the emotional life of your overweight child. Whenever you meet resistance or setbacks as you move down this healthy path, keep this in mind: The payoff may be years in the offing, when your child looks back and remembers that you cared enough to accept the incredible challenge of helping to redefine his image to one of good physical and mental health.

Here are the six steps of the rescue plan.

1. Be a coach, instead of a judge.
2. Go for the goal.
3. Recruit additional support.
4. Design a nutritional plan.
5. Organize an exercise effort.
6. Celebrate strengths.

Each step incorporates rescue techniques described in other parts of the book. This chapter will summarize and organize the techniques in accordance with the plan to help you stay on target. You will also want to return often to rescue techniques of the previous chapters for more details as you continue to encourage and guide your child.

STEP 1:
BE A COACH, INSTEAD OF A JUDGE

If your child is to embark on the goal of attaining a healthy lifestyle, she will have to view you as a coach rather than a judge. Whether you are a parent, a professional, or a concerned relative, your role as a coach is crucial. The first order of coaching is communication with your overweight child. You will need to be empathic and form an alliance with her in order to reach her effectively. You'll understand the concept of alliance better if you observe a good athletic coach.

Good coaches are enthusiastic, positive, and concerned. They convey a sense that they believe in the kids they coach. When you're a coach, you believe your children will do their best, and they know it. They feel like you're on their side. You can criticize, you can expect a lot, and children will accept the advice in the spirit of learning. As a coach, you can encourage good results, and your children will feel you trust and believe in them.

Coaching involves the right tone of alliance as well as the right words. Because coaching an overweight child can be frustrating, it is easy to find yourself impatient and angry. You might raise your voice, yell, or scold more than you would like. There's no sense in criticizing or becoming too hard on yourself. Your job is difficult, and sometimes even good coaches lose their tempers. Tell yourself, "Remember, I'm on her side, and this is difficult for her" or "I have to reassure him that I believe in his ability to learn to discipline his eating." Calm yourself and try again. Be sure to take some time every day to talk and listen to your child separately from other siblings so you can reassure her. Furthermore, to maintain a coaching attitude, conversations should not center only on weight. Your more general, loving interest in your child will communicate better that you care and are truly a coach.

In contrast, imagine the judges who are portrayed in courtrooms on TV, who determine whether a person is guilty or innocent and mete out punishments. When you're a judge, you're looking for your child's mistakes and are ready to punish her. When you act as a judge and not a coach, your child will assume that you expect her to fail. She'll feel intimidated or angry. She'll wonder, *What will the punishment be if I don't do my exercises or if I eat too much?* instead of *Mom and Dad will be pleased with me if I can keep up this good work.* Your child will feel like you're manipulating or

COACHING CONVERSATION

Mom: Caitlin, you know I've struggled with keeping myself at a healthy weight ever since I was about your age, and one thing I know for sure is that other kids are not very understanding of kids who are overweight. I really want you to be healthy, and I sure would hate it if your being overweight prevented people from getting to know you.

Caitlin: Mom, I'm not that fat, and I have friends. I don't think I have the problems you did.

Mom: Actually, I agree. You do have friends and you're only a little overweight, but after your last checkup Dr. Braun was concerned enough to bring it to my attention. She suggested that you lose about 20 pounds. I was thinking that we could work on this together. It would be good for both of us and will be a lot easier now because you don't have that much weight to lose.

threatening her, instead of helping and guiding her. When she exercises or eats properly, she'll expect her judging parents to say, "I told you so," which will make the overweight kid believe she's lost another argument.

Sometimes your child will still be defensive and resent you for intruding, even if you say the right thing as a coach. It's tricky because obviously your child must learn to accept constructive criticism and direction. If she's going to be successful at this enormous challenge, she'll have to learn to eat nutritiously and incorporate exercise into her daily activities. These changes will be easier for her to handle when they come from a coaching parent. Coaches inspire kids, and for that reason coaches can be powerful leaders. In this situation, establishing high expectations is positive and encouraging for children. It's also clear that the very same expectations can cause bitter battles and resentment when they come from parents who act as judges. Being patient during coaching will also help your child to be patient with herself. Patience is an important characteristic to develop for weight loss.

Caitlin: I don't eat that much now, and I hate it when kids are always talking about dieting. Besides, even if I did go on a diet, I bet I wouldn't lose any weight. I'm just destined to be chunky. It's in my genes.

Mom: If we do this together, I think we can be successful, and you'll be happier with yourself. It would also make shopping for summer clothes a little easier, for you and me. We can start slowly so we won't have to make too many changes. It won't be a diet as much as healthy nutrition. Now that spring is here, we could take walks in the park every day, and that would be fun and even give us time to catch up on each other's life. You don't have to decide right away, Caitlin, but just think about it.

Caitlin: Okay, Mom, I'll think about it. At least taking walks together might be fun.

Mom: I think this will help both of us. I found a book with some good ideas we could try. You can look through it when you have some time.

United Coaching and Power

When two parents are involved (and even three or four), the parents who are coaches and not judges will be most effective for changing children's inactive lifestyles to healthy ones. And the power of coaching is multiplied if children believe that their parents are powerful people. If one parent demeans another parent who coaches, children won't be as accepting of their advice. If parents demean themselves, their expectations will not be as influential to their children.

Parents who are coaches, like Caitlin's mother, can use one-on-one communication to show their children that they are on their side (see "Coaching Conversation").

Finding Other Coaches

Although one or both parents can be coaches, parents may benefit from outside assistance if family relationships about weight are already quite sensitive. As Jeff's case showed, a family physician who has a good relationship with your children could be effective. A sports coach may also be an excellent person to communicate with your child, as was true for Amanda. Another person to help you with your intervention might be your child's favorite teacher, as I suggested in chapter 4. Although it's always best for parents to communicate with their children, don't rule out the assistance of other important adults.

STEP 2:
GO FOR THE GOAL

Setting realistic goals can be quite different for overweight children than it is for overweight adults because children are at varying places in their growth and development. For some overweight children, weight stability rather than weight loss will be an appropriate goal because they are still growing and maturing. Actual weight loss may be more appropriate for very overweight children or for older adolescents who are no longer growing. You and your child should seek medical guidance on where to set his weight loss goals. A pediatrician or family doctor can determine where your child is on the weight chart for his age and size and confirm whether you should be concerned about overweight. You'll also require advice as to how long it should take for him to reach his long-term goal of a healthy weight. And it will help to set weekly targets and possibly give rewards when he accomplishes them. Your child will feel more successful if you set short-term weight loss goals that he can more easily achieve, rather than difficult goals that he will fall short of accomplishing. See "Grace Goes for the Goal" to see how one mother helped her daughter.

Emphasizing the Process

If you emphasize the *process* of healthy living, you can reward your child when she invests time in doing a certain amount of exercise each week or for staying on her prescribed nutritional plan. If she follows the appropriate eating and exercise guidelines, she will eventually attain her goal even if

GRACE GOES FOR THE GOAL

Fifteen-year-old Grace attributes the secret to her success to setting and meeting regular goals. When she came to terms with her overweight a year ago, Grace weighed 180 pounds and was 5 feet 4 inches tall. She had gone dress shopping for a wedding and couldn't find anything to fit. Frustrated with her overweight, she accepted her mother's suggestion to try Jenny Craig. At Jenny Craig, Grace learned how to make meal choices appropriate for her age and was encouraged to exercise regularly. She learned that a goal of 130 pounds was appropriate for her height. Being on the swim team, where she was required to swim 3½ hours a day, also helped her weight loss plan and has continued to keep her fit. It's taken Grace a year, but she now weighs 140 pounds and is very happy with her accomplishments.

Grace also had a lot of family support, especially from her mother, who helped her set short-term goals. She would take Grace shopping for some new clothes when Grace dropped a dress size. Sometimes she encouraged Grace to buy clothes that were a little too tight but that she could save to wear when she accomplished a new weight loss goal. Grace knew that if she continued to take weight off, she'd soon fit into the too tight jeans that were waiting for her.

In addition to swim team, Grace sings, plays the piano, and is a good student, with a 3.5 grade average. She would like to go to a 4-year college and hopes to become either a firefighter or a teacher. Although she admits she didn't have boyfriends when she was overweight, she's had a very nice boyfriend for the past 4 months. Grace's target goal is still 130 pounds, and with all her past successes, she believes she'll achieve her goal weight soon.

she doesn't lose weight every week. Emphasizing the process will prevent your child from feeling discouraged during those times when the scale doesn't show weight loss.

Some families like to establish contracts detailing the requirements and rewards of the health plan (see "Contract for a Healthy Start" on page 204), but such contracts are certainly optional.

CONTRACT FOR A HEALTHY START

Andrew, his mom, and his dad agree that they will all try to help Andrew lead a healthier lifestyle. Andrew will respect his parents' new guidelines for healthy eating and will exercise for at least 1 hour each day. Gym class and sports will count toward the hour of exercise each day. For each week Andrew stays within his food and exercise guidelines, his parents will award Andrew $10 toward his bicycle fund. When Andrew has saved enough money, he may purchase a bicycle of his choice.

This contract was agreed to on —————————, 200—

Signed by:

Andrew Starr, Terrific Kid

Alex Starr, Supportive Father

Melissa Starr, Supportive Mother

STEP 3:
RECRUIT ADDITIONAL SUPPORT

Although you may have already found other important people to assist you in communicating with your overweight child about his problem, you'll also want to provide continuing family, peer, and outside support while helping him change his habitual eating and inactive lifestyle.

Family Support

The recommendations in chapter 7 for changing family patterns must be a priority for encouraging overweight children to become physically fit. If you believe you have serious issues within your family dynamic that are encouraging weight gain or inflicting emotional pain on your child, you'll want to visit a psychologist to correct the underlying problems as well as attempt to change his weight problems.

Enlisting sibling support, while not always possible, is certainly worth the effort. A sibling can make a real difference in an overweight child's self-confidence. A parent could have a conversation with a brother or sister to encourage support (see "Sibling Support: A Sample Conversation" on pages 206–207).

Peer Support

If your overweight child has close friends, try to enlist their support as well. However, don't talk to your child's friends without informing your child first. Kids, especially adolescents, may prefer talking to their friends on their own, or they may want to keep their health plan private. Parents should honor their children's requests in regard to peer support.

Friends who are also involved in a health plan can supply the best kind of peer support. Adolescent Weight Watchers groups or therapy groups organized for the specific goal of weight loss help children to feel less lonely with their problems.

You may also wish to contact your child's school nurse or counselor to determine if the school is interested in initiating a health support group. Weight loss summer camps are also great opportunities to introduce your child to healthy eating and exercise in a fun environment. They can help kids know they're not alone with their problem. Consider what you learned in chapter 7 about how you can encourage appropriate role models for your child.

Overweight children will be encouraged by watching adults or other peers who lead healthy, active lifestyles, and support groups, summer camps, and weight loss groups give kids a chance to do so. The appendix lists resources for such support groups and camps.

STEP 4:
DESIGN A NUTRITIONAL PLAN

Your physician or a nutritionist recommended by your physician can help you design a nutritional plan for your family. Many effective nutritional plans offer a variety of approaches to healthy eating. Weight Watchers has its own nutrition plan, as do Jenny Craig and other adolescent therapy

SIBLING SUPPORT: A SAMPLE CONVERSATION

Dad: Will, I need to talk to you about something that's been on my mind for a while.

Will: Yeah, Dad. There's a great Brewers game on TV. Could we talk later?

Dad: I'm sorry, but this is too important to postpone. Your sister is really having a struggle with her weight. Although you're tough on Katie, I know you care about her, too, and we really need your help. Your opinion really means a lot to her.

Will: I know that, but she's so fat she looks like a blob. It's embarrassing to be around her. Why doesn't she just lose weight?

Dad: That's exactly what she's planning to do, but it's not so easy, and calling her a "blob" only makes it harder for her. It's going to take her a long time, and she's

groups. Teaching kids about appropriate portion size is also critical to healthy eating. You should serve meals from the kitchen so you can tailor portion sizes and get your child used to smaller servings. It's easy to take too much mashed potatoes if the bowl is passed around family style. Also, it's a good idea not to give children choices at your main meal. It's too easy for them to keep choosing macaroni and cheese every night instead of the nutritionally balanced dinner you've prepared. Unhealthy food shouldn't be among the regular options for any meal.

Regular family mealtimes and balanced, nutritious meals for losing weight all have to be incorporated into a healthy plan. Any weight loss program targeted toward children should give consideration to children's occasional need for treats. When you change your children's eating patterns, you will undoubtedly need to change your cooking and family eating habits as well. Of course, that will also improve your entire family's health! If your children show an interest in grocery shopping and in cooking for the family, going to need our help. We have a lot easier time with our weight than Katie or Mom, so I try to be considerate and patient, and I'm hoping you'll be kind, too. If you give Katie a little encouragement and tell her things like she's a smart, good person, or you're glad she's trying to lose weight and you want to help, I know she'll appreciate it. Maybe you could go for some bike rides with her to help her with the exercise or just let her know you notice when she loses weight. A few kind words from you would give her confidence. Right now she can't even imagine a boy ever liking her because of her weight. Will, the family just has to stick together, and it'll mean a lot to me if you help us out with Katie's problem.

Will: Okay, Dad, I can do that. I didn't think Katie even cared what I thought, but I guess you're right. Sometimes she even asks me how she looks. I suppose it is hard for her, and I'll try to help. So, you want to watch the game?

please encourage it as this is a great way to get them involved in nutritious eating.

STEP 5:
ORGANIZE AN EXERCISE EFFORT

Regular exercise works best if the whole family is involved, or if your children are involved in organized sports. There are many suggestions in chapter 5 to encourage your children's activities. I also want to reiterate the importance of setting limits for screen time as well as eating while watching television. Those two changes will be remarkably effective for your children's physical fitness. Making exercise into family play and fun will enhance your health plan and will also cement family relationships. Encourage your children to exercise for at least 1 hour a day.

DEBORAH IS ON HER WAY

Deborah's dad introduced her to me as "the person of the day" for our interview, and I could tell how proud he was of her. Deborah's mother encouraged her to participate in an interview for our book. Now 13, Deborah shared her story. Although she's 5 feet 6 inches tall and weighs 210 pounds, that's 15 pounds less than she weighed last year.

Deborah learned about nutrition at a weight loss camp her parents convinced her to attend during the summer. Deborah admitted that she didn't expect to like the camp, and her parents had to coax her to attend. She's glad she went because she learned a lot and even had fun.

Deborah's an A/B student, is enrolled in honors classes, and spends about 2 hours a night on homework. Her teacher has told her she's very creative. Deborah does public speaking, does needlework, and plays the piano. She also plays basketball and volleyball and for at least 20 minutes each night does the exercises she learned at camp. Deborah has just enrolled in a fitness group that meets 3 days a week to exercise. She thinks that will help her with her weight loss plan.

Deborah also has plenty of friends, and she says as long as kids know her, they're nice to her. It's when they don't know her that they may be put off by her weight. Kids don't taunt Deborah for her overweight, but she's sure that if they did, her friends would defend her. She admits she may not have as many boyfriends as other girls, but claims that doesn't bother her because she's had a few and most of her friends don't date yet. Kids in her class usually go together in groups to the movies or to someone's house, and she's always included. Deborah is pretty confident that she'll gradually lose weight and feels good now because she's successfully lost so much weight already.

STEP 6:
CELEBRATE STRENGTHS

In chapters 3, 4, and 5, I described how to celebrate your child's strengths. You'll have to make a true commitment to building your child's self-esteem, fostering her school achievement, and inspiring her interests and involvement. Being aware of your child's physical and sexual development in comparison with kids her age is essential for you so that you can provide the knowledge and psychological support she requires as she matures earlier or later or grows faster or more slowly than her peers.

Deborah's success story was encouraged by her parents, and you can inspire your own children's success stories (see "Deborah Is on Her Way").

Building Confidence despite Rejection Is Critical

If your child sets his own goals to eat healthier and exercise regularly, he will first need to believe that he is a good, smart, and talented young person and that his future can be bright. Children are desperate for their parents' reassurance in a world that fiercely rejects them because they are overweight. As your child progresses to an active lifestyle and a healthier weight, he will surely feel he has initiated the rescue of his own emotional life. Although we would all like to change our society to be more empathic toward and tolerant of those who are overweight, our first priority is our children's good health, and that will result in a more accepting world for our children.

LOOKING TOWARD
A HEALTHY FUTURE:
You Are the Key

Remember eighth-grader Alyssa from chapter 1, who wrote about having more hope for the future? With the intervention of a caring teacher, she realized that she could be hopeful about herself, her weight loss, and her life. You, too, armed with the advice in this book, can rescue your overweight child from the hopelessness in which he may be mired and help him look toward a healthy future.

Shifting your child's worldview from pessimism to optimism should be a key goal of yours. Many of the adults I interviewed, who were overweight as kids, still had emotional scars from childhood. The legacy of overweight can cast a lifetime shadow, which is why it's imperative that you start now to help your child develop a vision of the future that is hopeful and positive.

And make no mistake about it: How you treat your child and how you allow other adults to treat him can have a dramatic effect on his emotional life.

Both research and clinical experience point to the importance of adults' believing in children. That is, if we convey to children that we think there is something special about their abilities, children perceive it as a message to achieve and believe in themselves. In every family with more than one child, siblings compete for favored status, and competition within the family may steal children's internalized sense of optimism. Peers or negative experiences at school may also rob children of their confidence in their ability to accomplish their dreams. These potentially damaging factors, which fall outside your control, make it even more important for you to focus with a positive eye on your child in matters that you do have control over.

As I discussed in chapter 3, successful adults, particularly from my *See Jane Win* research, could point to people in their lives who had had a positive influence on them. Sometimes it was a grandparent, an aunt, a teacher, a minister, a sibling, or a Scout leader, and of course it was often a parent. For overweight Darlene, a successful adult I interviewed, although her mother and grandfather died by the time she was 5, memories of their incredible love for her continued to inspire her. She lived with her grandparents briefly after her mother died, and she has strong memories of her grandfather's having been totally delighted with her. Those memories help lift her to success despite many challenges.

There is no easy formula for inspiring an overweight child's resilience in light of his abuse by so many peers and adults. But you can and must believe in his ability to succeed despite disadvantages. In addition to your support, introducing him to other adults who have faith in him may be the best way to inspire your child to live up to his potential and overcome the emotional distress of his weight problem.

Even as this book goes to press, more and more attention is being paid to the epidemic of childhood obesity that is wreaking havoc on families across the country. Consumer products companies and fast-food chains have vowed to cut the fat content in their foods, which is certainly a step in the right direction. Some brave school districts are walking away from the rich contracts offered by soda and candy companies who vie for the unfettered right to peddle their products to schoolkids. You can support your schools and encourage them to substitute machines that sell low-fat milk drinks, healthy soups, or plain cold water. Other schools are putting physical education requirements back on the curriculum because parents like you care, so be sure your school knows your wish for school exercise.

Every piece of this campaign is important. Every victory helps to turn back the tide that stands to threaten the health of our nation. And yet the front line of this battle remains in homes like yours across America. You hold the key to both reversing the weight gains in your family and pro-

tecting the emotional life of your child as you address her physical condition. The war will not be won or lost in congressional hearings or school
board meetings, but rather in the loving homes like yours that nurture our
children's fragile emotions, and spark visions of a better future for them.

With your support and understanding of their psychological needs,
you'll be able to reverse your children's underachievement and encourage
successful achievement, convert their overeating to healthy eating, change
their passivity to energizing exercise, turn their lack of confidence to in-
spired belief in themselves, and finally and most profoundly, watch as they
grow into bright, active, healthy young men and women with a future full
of limitless opportunity and happiness.

APPENDIX

Weight Control Groups That Include Children

Childobesity.com
www.childobesity.com

Shapedown
www.shapedown.com/page2.htm

The Solution
www.thepathway.org

Slimkids
http://slimkids.com

Weight Watchers
www.weightwatchers.com

Internet Sites for Nutrition

Action for Healthy Kids
www.actionforhealthykids.com/html/main.htm

Centers for Disease Control: Overweight Children and Adolescents:
Recommendations to Screen, Assess, and Manage (includes weight charts)
www.cdc.gov/nccdphp/dnpa/growthcharts/training/modules/module3/text/page1b.htm

National Cancer Institute—5 A Day Program
www.5aday.gov

National Institute of Diabetes and Digestive and Kidney Diseases:
Weight Loss and Control
www.niddk.nih.gov/health/nutrit/nutrit.htm

Nutrition.gov
www.nutrition.gov

School-Based Nutrition Programs—Eat Well and Keep Moving
www.hsph.harvard.edu/nutritionsource/EWKM.html

Exercise Information and/or Weight Charts

Body Mass Index for Teens
www.cdc.gov/nccdphp/dnpa/bmi/bmi-for-age.htm

Medline Plus—Exercise for Children
www.nlm.nih.gov/medlineplus/exerciseforchildren.html

NutriTeen
www.nutriteen.com

Shape Up America!
www.shapeup.org

Weight Loss Camps for Kids

Alpengirl
Camps in Montana, Washington, Scandinavia, Hawaii, and Alaska
www.alpengirl.com

Camp Endeavor
Wisconsin Dells, WI
www.campendeavor.com

Camp Kingsmont
West Stockbridge, MA
www.campkingsmont.com

Camp La Jolla
La Jolla, CA
www.camplajolla.com

Camp Nu Yu
Wildwood, FL
www.campnuyu.com

Camp Pennbrook
Leonia, NJ
www.camppennbrook.com

Camp Rancheria
Yorkville, CA
www.camprancheria.com

Camp Shane
Ferndale, NY
www.campshane.com

Camp Timbercreek—Healthy Kids Camps
Lenoir, NC
www.healthykidscamps.com

Camp Xcel
Chula Vista, CA
www.campxcel.com

Champion Body's Sports Ministry
Lithonia, GA
www.championbodysfootball.com

New Image Camps
Camps in Lake Wales, FL; Pocono, PA; and Ojai, CA
www.newimagecamp.com

NOTES

INTRODUCTION

p. 2 [. . . children to be overweight . . .] Ogden, C. L., K. M. Flegal, M. D. Carroll, and C. L. Johnson (2002). Prevalence and trends in overweight among U.S. children and adolescents, 1999–2000. *JAMA: The Journal of the American Medical Association* 288 (14): 1728–1732.

CHAPTER 1

p. 6 [. . . dire public health consequences for our country . . .] Ogden, C. L., K. M. Flegal, M. D. Carroll, and C. L. Johnson (2002). Prevalence and trends in overweight among U.S. children and adolescents, 1999–2000. *JAMA* 288 (14): 1728–1732.

p. 7 [. . . receiving chemotherapy for cancer . . .] Schwimmer, J. B., T. M. Burwinkle, and J. W. Varni (2003). Health-related quality of life of severely obese children and adolescents. *JAMA* 289 (14): 1813–1819.

CHAPTER 2

p. 17 [. . . in the United States . . .] Wolf, A. M., G. A. Colditz (1998). Current estimates of the economic cost of obesity in the United States. *Obesity Research* 6: 173–175.

p. 17 [. . . severe health conditions . . .] Willett, W. C., W. H. Dietz, G. A. Colditz (1999). Guidelines for healthy weight. *New England Journal of Medicine* 341: 427–434.

p. 20 [. . . population was obese . . .] Flegal, K. M., M. D. Carroll, C. L. Ogden, C. L. Johnson (2002). Prevalence and trends in obesity among U.S. adults, 1999–2000. *JAMA* 288: 1723–1727.

p. 21 [. . . short time period . . .] Ogden, C. L., K. M. Flegal, M. D. Carroll, C. L. Johnson (2002). op. cit.

p. 23 [. . . 3.5 hours per day . . .] Gentile, D. A., D. A. Walsh (2002). A normative study of family media habits. *Applied Developmental Psychology* 23: 157–178.

p. 23 [. . . and quietly reading . . .] Klesges, R. C., M. L. Shelton, L. M. Klesges (1993). Effects of television on metabolic rate: Potential implications for childhood obesity. *Pediatrics* 91: 281.

p. 24   [. . . about 40 per week . . .] Schlosser, E. (2001). *Fast Food Nation: The Dark Side of the All-American Meal.* New York: Houghton Mifflin.

p. 25   [. . . and vegetables a day . . .] Krebs-Smith, S. M., A. Cook, A. F. Subar, L. Cleveland, J. Friday, L. L. Kable (1996). Fruit and vegetable intakes of children and adolescents in the United States. *Archives of Pediatrics and Adolescent Medicine* 150: 81–86.

p. 25   [. . . conducted in 2001 . . .] Centers for Disease Control and Prevention (2002). Surveillance Summaries, June 28, 2002. *Morbidity and Mortality Weekly Report* 51 (No. SS-4).

p. 26   [. . . obesity among children . . .] Berenson, G. S., S. R. Srinivasan, B. Weihang, et al. (1998). Association between multiple cardiovascular risk factors and atherosclerosis in children and adults. *New England Journal of Medicine* 338: 1650–1656.

p. 27   [. . . and blood sugar . . .] Chu, N. F., E. B. Rimm, D. J. Wang, H. S. Liou, S. M. Shieh (1998). Clustering of cardiovascular disease risk factors among obese schoolchildren: The Taipei Children Heart Study. *American Journal of Clinical Nutrition* 67: 1141–1146. Freedman, D. S. (2002). Clustering of coronary heart diease risk factors among obese children. *Journal of Pediatric Endocrinology and Metabolism* 15: 1099–1108. Schlundt, D. G., L. Herman, F. De Luca, D. R. Counts (2001). Evaluation of the insulin resistance syndrome in 5- to 10-year-old overweight/obese African-American children. *Diabetes Care* 24: 1359–1364.

p. 28   [. . . children are type 2 . . .] Zimmet, P. (2003). The burden of type 2 diabetes: Are we doing enough? *Diabetes-Metabolism Reviews* 29: 9–18.

p. 29   [. . . risk of early death . . .] Soren, N., C. Emborg, A. G. Molbak (2002). Mortality in concurrent type 1 diabetes and anorexia nervosa. *Diabetes Care* 25: 309–312.

Herzog, D. B., D. N. Greenwood, D. J. Dorer, et al. (2000). Mortality in eating disorders: A descriptive study. *International Journal of Eating Disorders* 28: 20–26.

p. 29   [. . . 106 had cancer . . .] Schwimmer, J. B., T. M. Burwinkle, J. W. Varni (2003). Health-related quality of life of severely obese children and adolescents. *JAMA* 289: 1813–1819.

p. 32   [. . . nutrition and public health . . .] Gortmaker. S. L., L. W. Cheung, K. E. Peterson, et al. (1999). Impact of a school-based interdisciplinary intervention on diet and physical activity among urban primary school children: Eat well and keep moving. *Archives of Pediatrics and Adolescent Medicine* 153: 975–983. Kavey, R. W., S. R. Daniels, R. M. Lauer, D. L. Atkins, L. L. Hayman, K. Taubert (2003). AHA Scientific Statement: American Heart Association guidelines for primary prevention of atherosclerotic cardiovascular disease beginning in childhood. *Circulation* 107 (11): 1562.

p. 32   [. . . essential vitamins and minerals . . .] Ballew, C., S. Kuester, C. Gillespie (2000). Beverage choices affect adequacy of children's nutrient intakes. *Archives of Pediatrics and Adolescent Medicine* 154: 1148–1152. Harnack, L., J. Stang, M. Story (1999). Soft drink consumption among U.S. children and adolescents: Nutritional consequences. *Journal of the American Dietetic Association* 99: 36–441.

CHAPTER 3

p. 38 [... sad, lonely, and nervous ...] Strauss, R. S. (2000). Childhood obesity and self-esteem. *Pediatrics* 105 (1): 1–5.

p. 39 [... craving for carbohydrates ...] Neville, K. (2003). Experts say food, mood linked: How to ease stress, beat the blues. *Environmental Nutrition* 26 (2): 1, 4.

p. 69 [... successful and happy lives ...] Rimm, S. B. (1995). *Why Bright Kids Get Poor Grades and What You Can Do about It.* New York: Crown Publishers.

p. 76 [... soothe sad feelings ...] Neville, K. (2003). op. cit.

p. 76 [... also low in calories ...] Rimm, S. B. (1995). op. cit.

CHAPTER 4

p. 78 [... their academic confidence ...] Rimm, S. B. (1995). *Why Bright Kids Get Poor Grades and What You Can Do about It.* New York: Crown Publishers.

p. 87 [... disorder and depression ...] Mustillo, S., C. Worthman, A. Erkanli, G. Keeler, A. Angold, and E. J. Costello (2003). Obesity and psychiatric disorder: Developmental trajectories. *Pediatrics* 111 (4): 851–859.

p. 91 [... diminish children's attention ...] Amen, D. G. (2001). *Healing ADD.* New York: Berkley Publishing Group.

p. 92 [... tests of mental development ...] Halterman, J. S., J. M. Kaczorowski, C. A. Aligne, P. Auinger, and P. G. Szilagyi (2001). Iron deficiency and cognitive achievement among school-aged children and adolescents in the United States. *Pediatrics* 107 (6): 1381–1386.

p. 92 [... counterproductive to learning ...] Collins, K. (2002, September 2). Can nutrition affect school performance? *AICR's Nutrition Notes*: 1–2. Available from www.aicr.org.

p. 105 [... learn better in school ...] Amen, D. G. (2001). op. cit.

CHAPTER 5

p. 109 [... elementary and secondary levels ...] Solinger, J. A student's involvement encourages good grades. *Iowa State University*, pp. 1–3. Available from www.public.iastate.edu; Phyllis Dykes & Associates, Inc., and Triad Research Group (2002). Comprehensive extracurricular activities program evaluation summary for school year 2001–2002. *Cleveland Municipal School District.* Available from www.cmsdnet.net.

p. 110 [... and school grades ...] Swanbrow, D. (1998, July 1). Teens who play sports get better grades. *Newswise: University of Michigan.* Available from www.newswise.com.

p. 112   [. . . sports and physical activities . . .] Faith, M. S., M. A. Leone, T. S. Ayers, M. Heo, and A. Pietrobelli (2002). Weight criticism during physical activity, coping skills, and reported physical activity in children. *Pediatrics* 110 (2): 1–8.

p. 116   [. . . to be overweight . . .] Eisenmann, J. C., R. T. Bartee, and M. Q. Wang (2002). Physical activity, TV viewing, and weight in U.S. youth: 1999 Youth Risk Behavior Survey. *Obesity Research* 10 (5): 379–385.

p. 116   [. . . ages of 14 and 16 . . .] Dowda, M., B. E. Ainsworth, C. L. Addy, R. Saunders, and W. Riner (2001, June). Environmental influences, physical activity, and weight status in 8- to 16-year-olds. *Archives of Pediatrics and Adolescent Medicine* 155 (6): 711–717.

p. 116   [. . . to be inactive . . .] VHA Inc. (2000, May 24). Weighty statistics. *Laurus-Health.com: Healthy Living.*

p. 116   [. . . reached adolescence . . .] National Heart, Lung, and Blood Institute (2002, September 4). NHLBI study finds dramatic decline in physical activity among African-American and White girls. *National Institutes of Health News Release.* Available from www.nih.gov.

p. 118   [. . . control body fatness . . .] Corbin, C. B., and R. P. Pangrazi (1998). *Physical Activity for Children: A Statement of Guidelines.* Reston, VA: NASPE Publications, 1–15.

p. 118   [. . . 3 days a week . . .] VHA Inc. (2000, May 24). op. cit.

p. 118   [. . . related to achieving higher grades . . .] Solinger, J. (2002). op. cit. Phyllis Dykes & Associates, Inc., and Triad Research Group (2002). op. cit.

p. 121   [. . . more television than that . . .] VHA Inc. (2000, May 24). op. cit.

p. 121   [. . . less than 4 hours . . .] Dowda, M., B. E. Ainsworth, C. L. Addy, R. Saunders, and W. Riner (2001, June). op. cit.

p. 123   [. . . to be overweight . . .] Eisenmann, J. C., R. T. Bartee, and M. Q. Wang (2002). op. cit.

p. 123   [. . . 600 calories a day . . .] Contrada, J. D. (2002, May 17). Family involvement key to helping children lose weight and keep it off. *Newswise: University of Buffalo.* Available from www.newswise.com.

p. 123   [. . . children's being overweight . . .] Dennison, B. A., T. A. Erb, and P. L. Jenkins (2002). Television viewing and television in bedroom associated with overweight risk among low-income preschool children. *Pediatrics* 109 (6): 1028–1035.

p. 124   [. . . fast-food restaurants . . .] American Heart Association (2002, April 24). Kids getting a steady diet of fast food on the tube. *American Heart Association: Meeting Report.*

p. 124   [. . . persuasive content . . .] Norton, A. (2002, April 16). Youngsters unaware TV ads are sales pitch. *Reuters Health.*

p. 134   [. . . learners in school . . .] Ogden, C. L., K. M. Flegal, M. D. Carroll, C. L. Johnson (2002). Prevalence and trends in overweight among U.S. children and adolescents, 1999–2000. *JAMA* 288 (14): 1728–1732.

CHAPTER 6

p. 137 [. . . during this phase . . .] Ripple, R. E., R. F. Biehler, and G. A. Jaquish (1982). *Human Development*. Boston: Houghton Mifflin Co.

p. 138 [. . . tenth-graders described themselves as overweight . . .] Grunbaum, J. A., L. Kann, S. A. Kinchen, B. Williams, J. G. Ross, R. Lowry, and L. Kolbe (2002, June 28). Youth Risk Behavior Surveillance—United States, 2001. *Morbidity and Mortality Weekly Report* 51: 1–64. Available from www.cdc.gov.

p. 139 [. . . indicated that they'd made efforts to lose weight . . .] Sweeting, H., and P. West (2002). Gender differences in weight related concerns in early to late adolescence. *Journal of Epidemiology and Community Health* 56 (9): 700–701.

p. 139 [. . . trying to lose weight . . .] Grunbaum, J. A., L. Kann, S. A. Kinchen, B. Williams, J. G. Ross, R. Lowry, and L. Kolbe (2002, June 28). op. cit.

p. 140 [. . . attributed to nutrition . . .] Ripple, R. E., R. F. Biehler, and G. A. Jaquish (1982). op. cit.

p. 140 [. . . girls in 1948 . . .] Herman-Giddens, M. E., E. J. Slora, R. C. Wasserman, C. J. Bourdony, M. V. Bhapkar, G. G. Koch, and C. M. Hasemeier (1997). Secondary sexual characteristics and menses in young girls seen in office practice: A study from the pediatric research in office settings network. *Pediatrics* 99 (4): 505–512.

p. 141 [. . . begun breast development . . .] Ibid.

p. 141 [. . . maturity on overweight . . .] Boodman, S. G. (1999, November 7). Girls and 'precocious puberty': Looking again at the age range. *The Seattle Times Company*, pp. 1–3. Available from http://archives.seattletimes.nwsource.com.

p. 141 [. . . 14 years of age . . .] Ripple, R. E., R. F. Biehler, and G. A. Jaquish (1982). op. cit.

p. 142 [. . . in sexual development . . .] Peskin, H. (1967). Pubertal onset and ego functioning: A psychoanalytic approach. *Journal of Abnormal Psychology* 72: 1–15; Peskin, H. (1973). Influence of the developmental schedule of puberty on learning and ego functioning. *Journal of Youth and Adolescence* 2: 273–290; Clausen, J. The social meaning of differential physical and sexual maturation. In *Adolescence in the Life Cycle*, edited by S. Dragastin and G. H. Elder, Jr. New York: Wiley, 1975; Livson, N. and N. Peskin. Perspectives on adolescence from longitudinal research. In *Handbook of Adolescent Psychology*, edited by J. Adelson. New York: Wiley, 1980; Petersen, A. C. and B. Taylor. The biological approach to adolescence. In *Handbook of Adolescent Psychology*, edited by J. Adelson. New York: Wiley, 1980.

CHAPTER 7

p. 169 [. . . on three variables . . .] Mussen, P. H., and E. Rutherford (1963). Parent-child relations and parental personality in relation to young children's sex-role preferences. *Child Development* 34: 589–607; Hetherington, E. M., and G. Frankie (1967). Effects of parental dominance, warmth, and conflict on imitation in children. *Journal of Personality and Social Psychology* 6: 119–125.

p. 187   [. . . within a year . . .] Irwin, M. L., Y. Yasui, C. M. Ulrich, D. Bowen, R. E.
Rudolph, R. S. Schwartz, M. Yukawa, E. Aiello, J. D. Potter, and A. McTiernan (2003).
Effect of exercise on total and intra-abdominal body fat in postmenopausal women.
JAMA 289 (3): 323–330.

p. 192   [. . . have weight problems . . .] Rimm, S. B. What's wrong with perfect? *Sylvia
Rimm on Raising Kids* 12 (4): 1–4.

CHAPTER 8

p. 199   [. . . believe in them . . .] Rimm, S. B., S. Rimm-Kaufman, and I. Rimm (1999). *See
Jane Win: The Rimm Report on How 1,000 Girls Became Successful Women.* New York:
Crown Publishers.

p. 200   [. . . lost another argument . . .] Ibid.

p. 200   [. . . act as judges . . .] Ibid.

p. 201   [. . . influential to their children . . .] Ibid.

INDEX

Boldface page references indicate charts and graphs. <u>Underscored</u> references indicate boxed text.